manifesting through meditation

manifesting through meditation

....

100 GUIDED PRACTICES TO HARNESS THE POWER OF YOUR THOUGHTS AND CREATE THE LIFE YOU WANT

Cassandra Bodzak

ROCKRIDGE
PRESS

Cover Designer: Rachel Haeseker
Interior Designer: Marietta Anastassatos
Art Producer: Hannah Dickerson
Editor: Brian Sweeting
Production Editor: Sigi Nacson
Production Manager: Jose Olivera

Textures © NKate/Creative Market, cover and p. I; all other textures used under license from Shutterstock.com
Author photograph courtesy of Kaysha Weiner Photography

Paperback ISBN: 978-1-63807-300-0
eBook ISBN: 978-1-63807-177-8
R0

In honor of Joan McDonald in heaven.

I would not be the most wonderful parts of who I am without your love and wisdom. You were in life and forever will continue to be my favorite angel.

I am certain that you were with me as I wrote this book, and I am grateful for your heavenly hand in it. Love you madly, Grandma.

contents

introduction

I'M SO HAPPY YOU HAVE FOUND YOURSELF HERE. This book holds the key to unlocking a whole new way of living in the world. You're here because, deep down, you, too, believe that you're capable of manifesting the life you dream of. Your soul knows that your ability to consciously bring your dreams into reality is as natural as breathing.

I'll show you the meditations, the wisdom, and the tools that transformed my life and the lives of countless others I've had the pleasure of working with. You'll gain the tools to have profound meditations that change the way you think, feel, and interact with the world. You'll learn how to listen to your intuitive instructions and get into earthly action toward fulfilling your dreams. Get excited! If you truly show up and use the meditations in this book as instructed, you'll ground that glorious future vision you have in your present-day reality.

How can I be so sure? Well, I've been testing and perfecting these methods for over a decade now. I've shown thousands of people from all over the world how to get out of their own way and become powerful manifesters in their life through my program Divinely Design Your Life: The Process—not to mention through countless workshops, meditation classes, and one-on-one sessions. You're in great company, and I'm ecstatic to welcome you to the club!

Perhaps the most powerful demonstration of the impact of this work is my own life. When I began my meditation and manifesting journey, I was in my early 20s—lost, stressed, working multiple jobs, barely paying rent, in a dead-end relationship, and feeling as if I was making a mess of what had felt would be a promising future when I graduated from college. I was at an all-time low. Life felt pointless, as if I were losing on all fronts. I desperately needed a shift. Can you relate at all?

I'll spare you the full memoir (you can read more about that story in depth in my first book, *Eat with Intention*), but here's the movie montage version: That moment set me on a mission to learn about meditation and spiritual principles, ultimately leading me to unlocking the power of manifesting in my life.

That's when the magic started happening. Little by little, I became happier and happier. I was able to look at situations in my life from a higher, more peaceful, and loving perspective. I began to follow what lit me up and prioritized work that brought me joy. You, too, have this to look forward to. Even before your manifestations come through, you'll notice that your life feels so much better!

I could regale you for pages with all the magical manifestations that have come into my life since that rock-bottom moment: my blog growing and attracting a bunch of coaching clients, producers from ABC finding a cooking video I had made and putting me on *The Taste* with Anthony Bourdain, and signing my first book deal within a year of committing to this work. Friends came into my life, I felt better in my body, mysterious pains disappeared—and I met my soon-to-be husband. Most important, I began to feel increasingly happy, joyful, and fulfilled. The possibilities are endless when you step back into your power and claim your ability to bring the vision you have for your life into reality.

I can't wait to guide you along your own magical manifesting journey with meditation. The most important thing: This is not a book to be simply read—this is a book that you need to *do*. I promise you can squeeze it into your busy life. You need only 10 to 30 minutes each day—not much if you think about it as time spent calling your vision for your life into reality, right? Show up for you, for your soul, and for your own peace and happiness.

The trickiest part may be getting started, so feel free to lean on the book bonuses at cassandrabodzak.com/manifesting. There, you'll find guided versions of some of the beginning meditations and some additional tools. This is a lifelong practice you're developing, so be easy on yourself. If you fall off for a day or so, just hop back on. If you're not quite hitting the sweet spot in a meditation, keep doing it for a week or two, and watch how your practice deepens each time you sit. Once you get into the groove, you won't want to stop. You'll be feeling great, and your life will be more magical than ever before.

....

an introduction to manifesting and meditation

A critical part of creating the life you want is believing that you *can* create the life you want. In this first section of the book, I'll demystify manifesting for you so you understand that this is part of your innate power as a divine being having a human experience. I'll also help you connect the dots around why meditation is the golden key in the conscious creation of your reality. By the end of this section, you'll be bursting with excitement to dive into the meditations, feeling confident that your consistent practice will yield life-shifting results!

What Is Manifesting?

Manifesting is our ability to be conscious creators of our lives. It's the practice of divinely designing your life, instead of falling victim to the circumstances around you or letting yourself get stuck in a cycle of reactivity to your outer environment. You can manifest anything you want—within our human biological limitations, of course (for example, you can't manifest a third arm!). Most people think of money when *manifesting* is mentioned, but that's such a small piece of this infinite pie. You can manifest relationships, opportunities, health upgrades, a baby, sunny weather on your wedding day, a job that brings you joy, a new puppy who loves to cuddle, your dream home, and beyond. You'll also find that manifesting positive emotions can be one of the most life-changing practices of them all. And, yes, you can consciously create the way you feel about your life as well. In fact, this is a process I recommend that all my clients do alongside their more goal-focused manifestations, because so often we want the things we do because of how we think we'll feel when they get here. The sky's the limit when it comes to manifesting.

How and Why Does It Work?

The first part of becoming a creator of your life involves what I like to call the magical, the divine, the heavenly. When we remember our true nature, we can create from it. We are divine beings, we are natural-born creators, we come from the infinite. Inside us lives our core essence—or soul—the energy of boundless love, infinite abundance, limitless possibilities. To become a powerful manifester, we must first connect consistently with our soul—and from *that place*, we must put out into the universe (or the quantum field) what we deeply desire to call into our lives.

The spiritual catchphrase "We have to get into alignment" refers to this very process. The way we show up for our lives is in accordance with the truth of our being, and meditation is the most powerful tool we have for this essential first part of manifesting.

The phrase "thoughts become things" is only a half-truth. The magic is in the belief. If you believe your thought deep within, it will show up in your reality. Your life now is a manifestation of the thoughts and beliefs you've had up until this moment. As you learn how manifesting happens, you'll begin to manifest the life you're dreaming of, instead of the life you have.

The first step of consciously creating your life involves going way below the conscious self—into the subconscious, into your divine essence—and shifting your fundamental beliefs about who you are, what you're capable of, and your worthiness to receive all that you desire. When you shift from the inside outward, your thoughts change, your actions change, and even how you feel about yourself changes.

The second part of the manifesting pie involves the "practical," or your aligned, earthly actions. We're living in a 3-D reality. Maybe the missing piece of your manifestation coming to fruition is for you to make a call, send an email, get on that dating app, or post a résumé. When we listen to and release our own judgments, we'll always be guided to our next aligned step forward. Taking action toward making our dreams and goals a reality every day puts us in places for our source to present us with the opportunities we're searching for.

The Benefits

We can use our manifestation skills to make life the adventure our souls have dreamed of! Manifestation opens us up to possibilities beyond what we thought was practical: a career that truly lights us up, projects we're most passionate about, and the confidence to shoot for the moon. We can also attract relationships that enrich our lives, experiences of a lifetime with the people we care about, and so much more. Manifesting makes tasks like buying a car, finding a home, or even going on your next vacation flow with more ease and magic.

Being a conscious creator of your life and consistently using your divine ability to manifest also make the journey so much more enjoyable. Life is supposed to feel fun, exciting, and joyful. It's not all sunshine and roses, of course; we all navigate grief, sadness, anger, and other difficult emotions during our time on earth. Having a manifestation practice isn't about bypassing our feelings when we're moving through hard moments: It's the rainbow that appears in the sky after the rainfall has let up. Our manifestation practice is a gentle love nudge, a reminder that while we're navigating those difficult times, we can still take our power back and create.

Manifesting teaches you a way of living in this physical world while reminding you that you are so much more. It allows you to touch the infinite, the divine, the magical in your everyday life—and that is priceless.

What Is Meditation?

Merriam-Webster's Dictionary defines *meditation* in four ways, all of which you will see are valid throughout our journey.

Meditate:

1. To engage in contemplation or reflection.
2. To engage in mental exercise (such as concentration on one's breathing or repetition of a mantra) for the purpose of reaching a heightened level of spiritual awareness.
3. To focus one's thoughts on; reflect on or ponder over.
4. To plan or project in the mind.

What qualifies as meditating is often based on which spiritual school of thought you belong to, and I love how *Merriam-Webster* leaves space for multiple interpretations. For me, meditation is when we go inside, connect to the truth of who we are, and allow ourselves to rest there for a bit. It can include a mantra, or we may do something specific with our breath, or even focus our awareness on a specific visualization in our mind's eye.

When I began meditating, I listened to all sorts of different guided meditations on YouTube, went to meditation classes at a Buddhist monastery in Brooklyn, received a mantra from my Vedic teacher, and earned yoga and meditation teacher certification from yet another lineage—and beyond. I tasted all the flavors to find what was best for me. Through the 100 meditations in this book, you'll discover many different ways to meditate—and the most important will be the one that works for you.

How and Why Does It Work?

All meditations work by quieting our "monkey mind," the mind that's connected to our limited consciousness of fear, limitations, and struggle, and reuniting us with our source, soul, or divine mind. At any moment, we're connected either to thoughts of our limited self or to thoughts of our unlimited self—we can't be connected to both at once. Meditation is the medium through which we can shift from our limited (or fear-based) mind into our unlimited (or love-based) mind.

Our fear-based mind is the mind that worries, that gets stressed and anxious, that thinks of all the ways things can go wrong, and so on. It's always making us the victim of our lives, depleting our energy and making us feel limited in what we can create. It involves the beliefs that we grew up with, from our family and lineage, and those that we acquired through different experiences in childhood. It also pulls from societal beliefs we adopted along the way from the media and from institutions we've interacted with. This is the mind that we quiet in our meditation practice; we free ourselves from these thoughts by simply closing our eyes, going within, and becoming the observer of our thoughts. In meditation, when we observe our thoughts, we're able to separate them from the truth of who we really are.

In meditation, we connect to our infinite mind, our source, our soul, or our divine essence. Whatever you prefer to call it, it's the quiet place, beyond all the noise, where we reunite with our limitlessness. Through our meditation practice, we build our muscles to return to this place time and time again, and we strengthen our connection with our infinite self. It's from this place that we remember our divine nature and connect to our higher consciousness and the infinite possibilities for our life.

The Benefits

Meditation has a cornucopia of benefits for us. It calms our mind and body, allowing us to take some deep breaths and connect back into our center. And the ripple effects are life-changing. Meditation not only helps us become a next-level conscious creator of our lives but also boasts significant, science-backed health benefits.

One of the most common reasons people come to meditation is for stress relief, and it's no wonder: An eight-week study of people practicing mindfulness meditation showed that it significantly reduces our biological stress response. With the epidemic of stress in our society, this benefit alone should be enough for anyone to "self-prescribe" a daily meditation practice for help managing stress!

Meditation even lulls stress's not-so-pleasant cousin, anxiety, into submission. That's right! Your daily sit can significantly reduce your feelings of anxiousness. Researchers studied the effects of various types of meditations, concluding that a wide range have a similar anti-anxiety effect and lead to better coping skills and less stress-related reactivity in longtime sufferers. I mean, how much more irresistible could meditation get?

Meditation has also been linked to alleviating depression and improving people's own beliefs as to how capable they are. The self-awareness you attain from a regular meditation practice impacts every area of your life. With your regular sit, you become increasingly able to recognize sabotaging thoughts and regulate your feelings, allowing you to show up as your highest self more often.

It's through all these amazing benefits of meditation that we can change our lives. We can wrangle our mind to work for us, instead of against us, and connect to the deepest part of ourselves to chart our course forward consciously.

So How Do Manifesting and Meditation Work Together?

Manifesting and meditation go together like the sun and the moon—they are a match made in living-your-best-life heaven! Meditation creates the solid foundation for our manifesting practice. It's the key to the door of our divine creative powers because it allows us to do the work on the deepest level possible, right at the core. Meditation is the path to reconnecting to the truth that we can create the life we want, allowing us to disconnect from our limitations and blocks, and quantum-leap into the future we've been dreaming about.

Let's break it all down into some easily repeatable steps so you can fully digest how the whole manifesting process works in connection with a consistent meditation practice.

We start off with a desire of what we want to manifest. The dreams, desires, and visions that you have for your life are not random. They are divinely connected to the very essence of your being, and they are unique to you. You may say, "Well, everyone wants love, money, health, and happiness"—and that's true. However, the qualities of how we want those elements to manifest in our lives will be vastly different for each of us. It's important to start our manifestation process by getting into our heart space, connecting with our soul, and becoming clear on what we're ready to call in. Don't worry, I've got 10 meditations to help you do just that in the "Meditations to Activate Your Heart's Desires" section ahead.

Once we have pinpointed our desire, it's important to break it down so we can understand it more deeply. We want to look at the three properties of our desires—as I like to call them in my signature course, Divinely Design Your Life—the overall life feelings (OLFs), the goals, and the genuine essence of the desire. I would highly recommend journaling on these questions:

- What are the overall life feelings that you imagine having when this desire is fulfilled?
- What are the tangible goals you would achieve that are interlaced with this desire?
- What is the genuine essence of the desire behind this manifestation?

We release the beliefs, limitations, and blocks in the way of calling it in. The main reason you haven't already manifested into reality everything you fantasize about for your life is that you have deep ingrained beliefs, limitations, and blocks that say you can't do, have, or be those things. I know that can seem a little harsh at first—like, ouch, I guess I don't believe in myself? Don't worry, we've all got the baggage of fears and negative beliefs that sabotage our manifesting efforts. We picked it up from our family, the media, society, some kid at school when we were younger, you name it. We were like sponges, soaking up the belief systems around us and absorbing them as our own. Slowly but surely, we forgot our magnificent, creative nature. You'll learn how to shake off and release these beliefs and blocks in the section called "Meditations to Release Fear and Limitations."

We embody the feelings, frequency, and characteristics of our future reality now. In the "Meditations to Embody the Future You" section, I have carefully curated practices to assist you in powerfully taking on this step of the process. You'll see exactly what the 2.0 version of you looks like, feels like, acts like, and beyond. You'll notice that the you who is already living your dream life has certain habits and rituals that you can incorporate into your life right now. You'll see the way they dress or how they move through their day with more joy, and you'll be able to make those changes now, too! There's so much magic when we take our earthly action to show up as the version of ourselves that we dream of—the person who creates a force field around us to attract the final pieces of the equation into our lives (like the new job, amazing partner, etc.).

We follow our divine guidance and intuitive wisdom to take co-creative action. Last, but certainly not least, we can't forget to do our part in the physical world after we complete our part in the energetic world of our meditation. Manifesting involves the practical and the magical. Your meditation practice is the solid foundation that directs your aligned actions for the rest of the day. We are co-creators with the universe, so we also must do our part. At the end of many meditations in this book, you'll find that I encourage you to receive any divine guidance that wants to come through. A few specific meditations are devoted solely to downloading these insights in different ways. A great habit to develop is to "ask for the next aligned step" at the end of any meditation practice.

Not all actions are created equal. It's so powerful when we allow our earthly action steps to come directly from a meditation because we want to take our cues from our divine essence. We want to receive our directions from infinite intelligence, from the field of unlimited possibilities. If we ask our conscious mind throughout the day, "What's the next step toward my goal?," chances are that our fear-based mind will respond. These actions aren't always bad, but they're often ineffective when it comes to our specific path. They waste our time because they lead us to behave in a standardized way—but you have a unique path. Your logical mind doesn't know what's right for you; it knows what's right for everyone.

How to Use Meditation to Commit to a Manifesting Practice

Meditation and manifesting go hand in hand. You'd be hard-pressed to manifest easily without a regular meditation practice. Allow your daily meditation practice to also be a commitment to your manifestation practice, even when your meditation isn't specifically about calling in a desire or visualizing your future. You'll still amp up your manifesting power by connecting to the place inside you that believes you can be, do, or have whatever your heart desires. By taking the time to sit, close your eyes, and spend some time in your divine essence—in the part of you that's infinite and connected to unlimited possibilities—you're turning yourself into a powerful magnet for all that you desire.

The time you allot every day to meditating can be a great time to check in with what you're manifesting. Take that postmeditation moment to sit in the feeling of it all already being yours, and give thanks for it before you start your day. Also, take this time to ask for the next aligned step, and journal whatever comes through. However long you decide to meditate, take these few moments afterward to solidify your manifesting practice.

ADDITIONAL TOOLS TO
BOOST YOUR PRACTICE

After teaching and guiding thousands of people in meditation over the years, I've discovered a plethora of different things you can have fun with to boost your practice or add extra oomph to your daily sit. Remember, none of these are necessary, so don't let them stop you from getting your meditation in!

A sacred space. Your sacred space can be as simple as a supportive chair with a plush blanket or as elaborate as a special cushion and mat you use only for meditation. The important thing is that you look forward to sitting there.

A meditation altar. This is not at all required, but I find it lovely to create a little altar for my meditation space. It can be a simple candle, crystal, and special picture in my hotel room when I'm traveling or the more elaborate altar in my nook at home.

Blankets. Having a blanket around can make your meditation that much cozier and allow you to focus on what's really important—relaxing into your infinite essence.

Eye covering. The beauty of an eye covering is that the darkness helps you dive deeper within.

Candles. Lighting a candle reminds us to connect to the light inside us. This practice has woven its way into many ancient spiritual and religious rituals because of its symbolism.

Crystals. Every crystal holds different properties and energy that can assist us, depending on what we're working on in our practice. Use amethyst to promote spiritual enlightenment. Rutilated quartz will help you clear any blocks to your desires. Use rose quartz to activate more love in your life. Green aventurine promotes manifesting opportunities.

Essential oils. Each essential oil has its own unique properties, which can assist in a myriad of areas we might be working on in our meditation practice. Use frankincense to bring deeper peace, allowing for an enriched meditative experience. Use lavender to cultivate feelings of relaxation. Clary sage helps us feel more balanced and creates stability to help us endure challenging times.

Herbs such as sage and palo santo. Burning of herbs has been used to clear negative energy and set the space for meditation for many centuries in Native American, Asian, and Middle Eastern traditions and beyond.

Solfeggio frequencies. I find these healing frequencies helpful to play during meditation because they assist in calming your mind and getting your body back into harmony (see page 79). A great place to start is at 528 Hz, known as the frequency of miracles and DNA repair.

Sound bowls. Many people enjoy listening to sound bowls during their meditation, finding that it helps them relax into a deeper place. It can be a helpful tool for beginning meditators who struggle with sitting in silence.

Physical activity. When we work out or exhaust our body in some way, we can much more easily slide into the quiet, peaceful, loving place we aim to get to in meditation. The physical exhaustion allows our body to stay out of the way so we can connect more deeply with our essence without much resistance.

Guided audio. If you struggle with self-leading during meditation, don't beat yourself up. It can be easier to listen to someone guiding you. For this reason, in the Resources section, I've included some guided recordings of a few meditations.

Moon cycles. The lunar cycles of the new moon and full moon (and astrology in general) give us opportune moments to tap into certain cosmic manifesting energies to supercharge our practice.

Q&A: Am I Doing This Right?

Do I have to meditate at a specific time of day?

You don't have to meditate at any specific time of day, but I suggest that you meditate as soon as you can after you wake up. The reason: You're more likely to get it done then, before you get caught up in your day. A great strategy is to find a time of the day that you know will work for your life and your schedule, and mark it in your calendar as time for meditation. The best time is always the time you'll consistently do it!

Do I have to meditate every day?

Meditation has so many benefits! But if life gets busy and you don't follow your routine for a day or two, jump right back in. If your schedule is too crazy one morning, try to squeeze it in before bedtime, or do it the next day. Don't treat your meditation ritual like the kind of diet where you fall off the program for a day or two, and then let it all go. Meditation will always be there for you the next day. In the grand scheme of things, it's more important for you to keep coming back to it, and meditate more days than not.

How long do I have to meditate for? Should I meditate twice a day?
A common recommendation is to meditate twice a day, once in the morning and again in the afternoon. I love meditating multiple times a day when I can. But, for now, focus on getting consistent with one time a day. If you feel the urge to meditate later on, go for it!

As for how long, start with what you can do consistently. (Ten 5-minute meditations are included in this book to get you started.) If you can only commit to 5 minutes right now, that's fine. Try to do 5 minutes every day for a month; next month, stretch this to 10 minutes, then 20 and beyond. For now, aim for consistency.

What if my mind wanders?
That's totally fine! You're not a bad meditator if your mind wanders—you're human! Mind-wandering is a completely natural part of the process. You'll find that some days will be easier than others for you to lasso your mind. Don't beat yourself up! Just gently bring your mind back on track when you notice it wandering, and continue on.

How do I know if I'm manifesting properly?
You'll know that you're manifesting properly when you start feeling more excited and joyful in your life and about your future. This signals that your belief has shifted to acknowledge that your future is coming. Before you know it, you'll start seeing little signs, opportunities, and synchronicities that affirm that your manifestation is on its way. Be patient with yourself. If you're showing up for your manifesting meditation practice every day, it's working for you, and you'll see the effects soon enough!

How important is it for me to be very specific about what I want when I'm manifesting?
It's more important to be open to all the options and the possibility of something even better than you imagined, as opposed to being married to a very specific version of the manifestation. It's okay to desire a certain specific job, or a person for a relationship, or a house—but always add, "This or something even better." This leaves the universe space to deliver something that is in your highest good, not just what your limited mind thinks it wants.

How fast can I expect manifestations to start appearing?
This will be different for everyone. It's completely based on what
you're manifesting and the blocks and beliefs you have regarding it. To
build some confidence, play around with manifesting something small
that you absolutely believe is possible (but that would still be pretty
magical!): tickets to a concert, a free lunch, a parking spot right outside
the supermarket, or a bouquet of flowers, for example. It may seem
silly when you've got such big dreams to call in, but this approach can
show you just how powerful you are, helping you build up confidence
for manifesting your larger desires.

**My romantic partner or business partner doesn't believe in mani-
festing or meditation or isn't willing to do this work with me. Can
I still manifest an outcome for both of us?**
Absolutely! You can manifest positive things for a partnership, even
if you're the only one doing the manifestation work. Avoid trying to
force them into this work if you've brought it up to them and they're
not ready. You don't want your partner to interject any negative beliefs,
or their own perceived limitations, in your head. Simply do the work
yourself consistently, and soon they'll be asking you, "What's changed?"
They'll be in awe of the positive shifts they've seen in you. When you
lead by example, you'll make them a believer without ever having to
convince them of anything.

How to Use This Book

If you're new to meditation, work your way through the first ten
5-minute meditations to get into the groove of a daily practice. Find a
time that will consistently work for you so it will become a natural part
of your schedule. If you've meditated before, skip to the first longer
meditation section, "Remember Your Power" (page 30), to begin your
journey.

Trust the process. The first four full-length meditation sections
will allow you to hit all the different angles of the four main steps in

the manifestation process. Go through those first four sections in order ("Remember Your Power" through "Embody the Future You"). From there, seek out the more specific categories that resonate with you. The meditations in "Manifesting Miracles, Synchronicities, Magical Opportunities" are a great follow-up to "Embody the Future You" if you want to keep it more open.

Once you've gone through the process, how you proceed is up to you. Do the meditation you're called to each day. Trust that the universe knows what you need. You can't go wrong with any of the meditations in this book! Sometimes those we're reluctant to do are just the ones that will pack the greatest punch. If a manifestation feels stalled, see the "Release Fear and Limitations" meditations for help. If your self-confidence has taken a hit recently, head over to "Remember Your Power." Not feeling connected to the life you're manifesting? "Embody the Future You" might have the meditation that will hit the spot. Just ask yourself, "What meditation would feel like the medicine for my heart today?" Trust where you're guided.

Finally, if a certain meditation resonates with you, and you find yourself going deeper, keep going. If you truly want to master a meditation, try doing it for **30** days straight. This will take your experience to a whole new level. If you're guided to commit to one in particular, chances are, there's something important there for you. Trust your inner guidance and take it on fully.

Allow this book to be your manifesting meditation handbook. Keep it in your bag, toss it in your suitcase, fill it with bookmarks or sticky notes. The tools and meditations in this book will work to the degree that you work them. They will continue to enrich your life, amp up your manifesting power, and support you in leading the life you once only dreamed of.

Let's Get Started

Finally, the time is here! It's your moment to start putting all this new knowledge to work for you as you begin to create the life you've been dreaming of. Remember: Knowledge is great, but what will truly change your life is how you show up from here on out. Will you create space for a daily meditation practice to help you manifest this next level of your life? I certainly hope you will! Dive into one of the 5-minute meditations right now to get the momentum going. Then slowly work your way through the meditations in the book each day. I've specifically curated them so that you can just sit back, meditate, and allow the process to work for you. I can't wait to see what you're about to create for your life!

PART II

100 meditations for manifesting

In this part of the book, we'll take all the concepts and principles of manifesting that you just learned and give you the real-life experience of doing the work to create the life you want. The 100 meditations in this section are here to help you remember your innate power, clarify what your heart truly desires, clear out any fear or limitations standing in your way, and embody the future you! You'll also find many meditations that are helpful for specifically manifesting certain desires, such as radiant health, fulfilling relationships, financial abundance, and more. Start with the first meditation and work your way through day by day.

5-Minute Meditations to Get Started

1. Connecting to the Heart

We will bring our awareness to our heart and practice opening up this powerful energy center to allow feelings of love, trust, and joy into our body. Connecting to your heart will help you make more love-based choices throughout your day, expediting your manifestation journey.

🕐 5 minutes

1. Sit in a comfortable position and close your eyes. Begin breathing deeply in through your nose and out through your mouth. Allow your awareness to turn inside, and release any distractions from the day.

2. Bring your awareness down to your heart center. Envision a bright ball of light there, glowing and expanding more and more with each breath.

3. Feel the feelings of your heart center as you breathe, tapping into unconditional love, acceptance, deep truth, and wholeness.

4. Allow your feelings to grow and that bright ball of heart-centered energy to expand until it encapsulates you in a ball of light around your body.

5. Rest here, and enjoy this feeling as long you like. Allow the light and love to recalibrate every particle of your body. Surrender and relax into this nourishing state.

6. When you're complete, bring your awareness back into your body and back into the room. Gently open your eyes.

2. Centering Breath

We all know what it's like to feel "off center," and not a lot of good comes from that place! This meditation is great in all sorts of situations to quickly bring you back into your power so you can make the most aligned choices for your day. You can do this meditation sitting down or standing up, for example, if you need to recenter before entering a big meeting, going on a first date, or giving a speech.

🕐 5 minutes

1. Close your eyes and place your hands on your heart. Start taking some deep breaths. Allow the distractions around you to slowly disappear as you focus on your breath.

2. Breathe in through your nose for a count of 4.

3. Hold your breath for a count of 4.

4. Exhale through your nose for a count of 4.

5. Try to quiet your mind by keeping your focus simply on the 4 counts of breath. Repeat for the next few minutes as you feel your nervous system recalibrate and relax.

3. Present Moment Power

We have no power when we're stuck in our past or too focused on worrying about the future. In the present moment, we have the ability to create our reality, and we have the power to change our lives. This meditation will help you come back to the present when you've been future-stressing or past-lamenting.

🕐 5 minutes

1. Get yourself into a comfortable position, eyes closed and spine elongated. Start taking deep breaths, in through your nose and out through your mouth. Notice how your body is feeling right now.

2. Bring your awareness to your breath. Notice the temperature in the room, the sounds of the room, the energy of the day. Don't judge any of it—just take note of what it is.

3. Call back any parts of you that are stuck in the past or worrying about the future. Bring them back to this present moment. Silently repeat in your head, "I am here now."

4. Set the intention, "I am willing to accept the present moment's power." Allow yourself to sit with your breath for a couple minutes longer, receiving whatever guidance, knowledge, or observations may arise.

4. Coming Back to Gratitude

Oops, did you end up in funky town? Fell off your horse of good vibes and now just feel kind of "bleh"? This meditation is an easy way to bring you back into your most magnetic energy by refocusing your thoughts on what you're truly grateful for in your life. When we embrace an energy of gratitude, we tap into the abundance that already exists in our current lives, and we call in even more for the life we're creating.

🕐 5 minutes

1. Close your eyes, get into a comfortable position, and start taking some long, deep breaths.

2. On each exhale, allow any tension that you're holding in your body to release. Continue until you feel deeply relaxed.

3. Take a few deep breaths, feeling the gratitude you have for simply being alive, for all that your body does for you each day to keep you breathing, moving, and living your life.

4. Begin to think of a loved one, a family member, a friend, or even a pet whom you feel tremendous love and gratitude to have in your life. Allow yourself to spend a few breaths really soaking in your love for this person or creature in your life.

5. Now expand it even further. What are you grateful for today? Keep it simple. Maybe you're grateful that it's a sunny day, or because you get to talk to your grandma on the phone later, or for the delicious lunch you had. Or maybe you're just grateful that you gave yourself these 5 minutes to meditate!

6. Allow all the little and big things you're grateful for to flow into your mind. Give each its moment. Fully appreciate it and breathe into it.

7. When you're ready to close, either put your hands in prayer position, or place one palm over the other on your heart. Take a deep inhale and exhale while saying a big "thank-you" silently to yourself.

5. My Best Self

Everyone who is manifesting has one thing in common: The life they want to live involves becoming the best version of themselves. Showing up as our best self every day is the greatest manifestation hack you'll ever learn because it opens up new portals of possibility in every aspect of your day. You may find that when you show up as your best self, much of the life you're ready to call into being can exist right now.

🕐 5 minutes

1. Find a comfortable position to sit or lie down (make sure you can stay awake!). Allow your body to relax and your eyes to close as you bring your awareness to your breath.

2. On each inhale and exhale, feel your body and mind surrender more to the breath. Allow any thoughts or tension to just float away, like clouds, on every exhale.

3. Set an intention to call on your best self, your highest self, the part of you that is divine, limitless, connected to source/the universe/ God/infinite love (whatever you resonate with). Breathe deeply as you open up to this connection.

4. Now bring your awareness to your third eye. This is located just between your eyebrows and an inch higher. Imagine a projector screen in front of you, and watch as your third eye projects a movie of you showing up as your highest self today in the situations ahead of you.

5. How are you handling the tasks, people, and situations as your highest self? What are you saying? What are you doing? How are you being? Allow yourself to simply be the observer, soaking it all in.

6. When you feel complete, simply return your awareness to your breath, and come back into your body. Bring yourself back to the room. Start stretching, and open your eyes when you're ready.

7. Now go take action as your best self!

6. Aligning Your Energy Centers

So much of being a powerful manifester of your reality is about alignment and finding harmony with the infinite within you. Our energy centers—sometimes referred to as "chakras"—correspond with different organs in our body, different feelings, and different characteristics and parts of the manifestation process. For this first beginner meditation, we'll simply allow ourselves to focus on the colors and alignment of these centers. (A more advanced version for you to build up to will come later.)

🕐 5 minutes

1. Find a comfortable position (sitting or lying down) and close your eyes. Allow your breath to bring your body to a space of relaxation and surrender before moving to the next step.

2. Bring your attention to your first energy center. This is at the base of your spine, where your sit bone hits your chair. See a beautiful, glowing ball of red light here. Watch it grow bigger and brighter with each breath.

3. Once you've made your first energy center bright and vibrant, it's time to move on to the second energy center, about six inches below your navel. Envision a gorgeous ball of deep orange light at this center, and allow your breath to make it expand and glow even brighter.

4. Next, move up to your third energy center, right at your navel. See a radiant yellow ball of light at this energy center. Watch it grow brighter and bigger with each breath you send to it.

5. Now move up even higher, to our fourth energy center, located right at our heart center. Notice its revitalizing, emerald-green light growing larger and more radiant with each breath.

6. Move on to the fifth energy center, located in the center of our throat and glowing with bright, sapphire-blue light. Breathe into this center and watch it expand and shine even brighter.

7. Keep moving upward, to your sixth energy center, located at your third eye. This is the space about an inch above the area between your eyebrows. Take in the lovely deep indigo–purple ball of light. Once again, send your breath there to help it thrive and radiate even brighter.

8. Finally, bring your awareness to your seventh energy center, the crown of your head. As you see a glowing ball of purple-violet light, allow your breath to help it grow even bigger and brighter.

9. Now see all seven of your radiant energy centers glowing with their rainbow of colors. Soak this in. Take a deep breath and hold it in, locking in this alignment. Gently bring yourself back into your physical body and into the rest of your day.

7. Divine Peace Is Mine

Our manifestation plans tend to go awry when we switch from being the creators of our life to reacting to everything that's going on. We know we've lost our power when we know we've lost our peace. This simple meditation will bring you back to peace and back into your creatorship.

🕐 5 minutes

1. Get into a comfortable, seated position with your eyes closed and your palms facing up. Start taking some nice, deep, grounding breaths.

2. Press both of your thumbs into your pointer fingers and silently say "divine" in your head.

3. Press your thumbs into your middle fingers and silently say "peace" in your mind.

4. Press your thumbs into your ring fingers and silently say "is" in your mind.

5. Finally, press your thumbs into your pinky fingers and silently say "mine" in your mind.

6. Keep repeating this process, tapping your fingers to your thumbs in this way as you repeat the mantra "Divine peace is mine."

7. In just a few minutes, you'll feel significantly more calm, relaxed, and, yes, peaceful. Finish with a deep breath in. Hold it for a moment as you repeat "Divine peace is mine" in your head, and exhale.

8. Expanding Your Magnetic Field

We are living magnets. Our heart's magnetic field can be detected up to three feet in each direction from our body. Pretty amazing, huh? Now that you're ready to magnetize all those beautiful desires of yours into your life, something helpful to do each day is to simply expand your own magnetic field. Use this quick 5-minute meditation to get you going!

🕐 5 minutes

1. Sit or lie down in a comfortable position and close your eyes. Begin taking long, deep breaths, in through your nose and out through your mouth. Allow your body to relax.

2. Bring your awareness to your heart center, and connect to its radiant ball of golden light. Breathe in and out, expanding and awakening this center of our magnetic field.

3. As you continue to breathe, watch the golden ball of light from your heart grow larger and larger. Feel your magnetic field expand.

4. See yourself as a magnet and feel like a magnet, attracting all the opportunities, situations, and circumstances that you've been dreaming about into your life. See your desires flowing to you, magnetized from your heart center.

5. Enjoy this feeling for as long as you like, and then close with a deep breath in through your nose. Hold it in. Fill yourself up with tremendous gratitude for all that's on its way. Exhale through your mouth, and open your eyes.

9. So Hum Meditation

So hum is a Hindu mantra that means "I am She/He/That" in Sanskrit. In Vedic tradition, it means identifying oneself with the universe or ultimate reality. It's a great mantra to remind yourself of your connection to the universe and a simple practice you can use when you have only a few minutes.

🕐 5 minutes

1. Get seated in a comfortable position with your palms on your lap, facing up, and your back straight. Close your eyes and begin taking some deep, calming breaths, in through your nose and out through your mouth.

2. When you're ready to begin, on the inhale, silently say "so" in your mind; on the exhale, say "hum."

3. Continue with this breath and silent mantra for a few minutes: "so" inhale, "hum" exhale. If your mind wanders, just gently bring it back to the mantra.

4. When you're ready to wrap up, take a nice, deep breath and hold it; say a prayer or set an intention, and then powerfully exhale.

10. Peace and Love

This meditation is a great recalibration when you feel stressed, fearful, or overwhelmed. It simply brings you back to love and peace. You can do it while walking or even at your office. (Of course, you can also do it in a traditional meditation format.)

🕐 5 minutes

1. Get into a comfortable position at home, at your desk, or while walking. Gently close your eyes (if you're at home!) or adopt a soft focus (if you're at work or walking), and bring your attention to your breath.

2. Take a few deep breaths to ground you in the present moment and relax your body. Allow the breath to begin to release any tension you may be feeling.

3. Begin to imagine that during every inhalation, you're taking in peace like air. Drink up the feeling of peace, and feel it coming into your body. Each time you breathe out, imagine that you're exhaling love—you're sending out love through your breath to all those around you, to loved ones, to the world, and beyond.

4. Continue this peace and love meditation for a few minutes, or until you notice a shift in how you're feeling.

Meditations to Remember Your Power

The meditations in this section will help you unlock the truth of who you are, a divine creator. Each meditation has its own unique way of bringing you back to the infinite truth of your being. It's from this space that we're able to manifest whatever we desire.

11. I Am a Divine Creator

This meditation uses a very simple phrase to go deep into your subconscious like a mantra and activate the truth within. Repeating this phrase is so powerful because when we're connected to our essence in meditation and then hear the truth, we recognize it deep within us.

🕐 **10–30 minutes or more**

1. Get into a comfortable position. Close your eyes and place your palms faceup in a receiving gesture. Begin by taking long, nourishing breaths.

2. Allow the breath to calm and center you in this moment. Exhale any stress or tension, and, as you inhale, feel your heart open. Continue this breath for a minute or so, until you find yourself in a nice, relaxed state.

3. Now gently bring in the phrase "I am a divine creator." Silently repeat it in your head, like a mantra. Allow the phrase to feel as if it's circling around your body, enchanting you and bringing you deeper into your own being. Continue for 10 to 20 minutes.

4. Slowly release the phrase, and bring your awareness back to the breath and back into your body. Gently stretch, and open your eyes when you're ready.

5. Optional: Take advantage of the state you're in by journaling or asking to receive any higher guidance on your next steps.

12. Connecting to the Cosmic Ocean

This meditation will begin your journey of getting out of your limited physical reality and diving deeper into the creation space. It's a powerful reminder of the infinite abundance and opportunities available to us in any moment.

🕐 10–30 minutes or more

1. Sit in a comfortable position with your eyes closed. Breathe only through your mouth. Allow your breath to flow in and out like the ocean—a wave coming into shore as you inhale, and then exhale, like the tide taking it back to sea. Allow each inhale and exhale to relax you into a deeper and deeper surrender.

2. Bring your awareness to your heart center. Imagine your awareness diving into a warm, loving, infinite ocean in the center of your heart.

3. See this infinite ocean all around you. Feel yourself floating in it, and allow your awareness of your body to melt away so you feel at one with the ocean.

4. Notice that this ocean—that you're a part of—goes on forever. Bring to your awareness the infinite possibilities and potential in this space. Allow yourself to simply rest in this awareness. Let yourself soak it up.

5. When you feel complete, gently bring your awareness back to your breath, and then back into your body. Allow yourself to slowly open your eyes. Step into the day with this experience alive within you.

13. Plugging into Creation Energy

One of the most powerful experiences you can have involves plugging into source or creation energy—also known as the energy that has created the entire universe. By using our meditation to plug in, we're coming home to the infinite material that we're made of. It's through this recognition that we reclaim our power and our ability to create.

🕐 **10–30 minutes or more**

1. Find a comfortable position. Allow your body to relax comfortably, and close your eyes. Begin taking some deep breaths to center yourself into your own energy.

2. Let your breath help your mind and body surrender even deeper, until you feel as if the physical world has melted away and you're one with your breath.

3. Imagine a ball of golden light emanating from your heart center. Let it grow and expand until you feel this light in every particle of your being.

4. Envision a column of light coming out of your heart, through your neck and your third eye (the space about an inch above the area between your eyebrows), and then out your crown, continuing upward to plug into the source or creation energy.

5. Feel this light beam from your heart plug into the sun like a ball of light of source. Feel the powerful connection—the electricity, the warmth, the love, the infinite intelligence, and whatever else arises for you from this encounter. Stay here, breathing and receiving for as long as you'd like.

6. When you're ready, draw that column of light back down into your heart center. Breathe there for a minute, integrating your experience back into your body before opening your eyes.

14. Observing Your Thoughts

When we become the observer of our thoughts, we realize that we are not our thoughts. This powerful "ah-ha!" allows us to more subjectively assess which thoughts we want to believe and put our manifestation power behind.

🕐 10–30 minutes or more

1. Get into a comfortable, seated position, eyes closed and back straight. Begin to place your focus on your breath, and relax your body.

2. Notice what thoughts naturally effervesce to the surface as you simply breathe and observe.

3. Become aware that you are not the thoughts—you're actually the witness of these thoughts. Allow each thought to pass by like a cloud after it has been brought to your attention.

4. Next, play around with *deciding* if you want to keep or discard each thought that arises. Continue with this practice for another 5 to 10 minutes.

5. Bring your awareness back to your breath. Feel it integrating this new truth about your thoughts and yourself. Gently complete your meditation, and open your eyes when you're ready.

15. Unstoppable You (Walking Meditation)

A walking meditation may be somewhat untraditional, but it brings with it incredible power. When you're walking as your unstoppable self, you'll bring the feelings of your power and remembrance of your truth into your physical body. This will enable you to anchor your divine truth further as you move through your daily life.

Tip: Do not do this meditation when you have to cross the street. It's ideal on a park path, on the beach, or any place where you can safely walk for a distance without being very alert.

🕐 10–30 minutes or more

1. Begin standing with your hands on your heart. Close your eyes, and allow your breath to help you tune into the energy of your heart center.

2. Feel yourself connecting to this heart-centered truth of who you are, your infinite power and potential. Allow yourself to spend a couple minutes here until you feel that you've locked into this space.

3. Open your eyes and begin walking straight ahead with your eyes on the horizon *as your unstoppable self.* Allow the feelings of your unstoppable self to flood your body as you move.

4. Notice how this version of you feels in your body. What kind of thoughts do you have? What possibilities are now available to you?

5. Continue walking in this energy for another 10 to 20 minutes. Put on some empowering music if that helps you get into the flow.

6. When you're complete, stop and stand in place. Put your hands back on your heart, and fill yourself with the gratitude you have for yourself—for the possibilities of your life and for how good you feel in this moment. Open your eyes and walk into your day when you're ready.

16. Self-Love Meditation

If we want to step into a life that truly lights us up, we need to have the fundamental building block of loving ourselves, just as we are now. From self-love, we can distinguish what our soul truly desires and create a life that makes us happy—not just one that we see everyone else wanting or having.

🕐 10–30 minutes or more

1. Get into a comfortable position and close your eyes. Begin connecting to your breath and relaxing your body.

2. In your mind's eye, imagine someone you love dearly. This could be a family member, a partner, a child, your best friend, or a pet—someone who makes it easy for you to tap into the immense love you have for them. Once you have them in mind, allow yourself to breathe into this love. Spend a few minutes feeling the love you have for them.

3. Now allow an image of yourself to replace their image. See if you can continue that feeling of immense love while looking at your own image. Think of everything you've been through, all the hard work you've put in, how kind you are—any of the things you're proud of yourself for. Feel that love. Spend 5 to 10 minutes here.

4. Begin breathing in through your nose, receiving love from this vision of yourself. Then exhale, sending love to this vision of yourself. Continue until you feel this inhale and exhale of love between the two of you fill up the room.

5. Take a deep breath in to fill yourself up and lock in all this self-love. Hold it for a moment, and then exhale, bringing that love into your day.

17. Sunrise/Sunset Meditation

During some of the darkest, most confusing, or lost times of my life, this meditation and the power of a sunrise or sunset have brought me back to my truth and reminded me of the divine's bigger plan for my life. When we allow ourselves to pause and see the natural rhythm of nature, we remember the divine rhythm in our own lives.

🕐 20–30 minutes or more

1. Get to a place where you can view the sunrise or sunset. Arrive 20 to 30 minutes before the actual sunset or sunrise to give yourself time to get situated and in a comfortable, seated position. (You can also do this meditation with a video of the sun rising or setting.)

2. Once you're settled, interlace your hands with your thumbs touching and place them on your lap. This mudra (hand gesture) will help synchronize the two sides of your brain while you mindfully observe the sun rising or setting. Keep your eyes open and gently focused on the horizon line.

3. Begin taking some conscious breaths, getting back into your body and your energy. Release any stress, tension, or external distractions. Allow your focus on the horizon line, along with your breath, to lull you into an almost trancelike state. Just be here, and allow any thoughts that arise to float by.

4. Allow yourself to witness this wonderful cycle of nature—how certain it is that, every day, there will be a sunrise and a sunset. On even the worst of days, the sun will still be on its path. Reflect on how this applies to your life—that you, too, are like the sun, one of the beautiful creations of the universe. You also get a fresh opportunity every morning to start anew, show up as your best self, and create the life of your dreams. With each sunset, you have an opportunity to release the day, learn from your mistakes, savor your successes, and know that tomorrow is another day.

5. Sit with this as you watch the sun fully rise or fully set. Keep yourself present with your breath, relaxed and surrendered to the connection you feel with the universe in this moment.

18. Ray of Light Meditation

"Be the light" is a way of saying, "Remember to be your highest self" or show up as your true essence. When we show up as our light, we literally brighten our lives and the lives of everyone around us. Taking time to tap into your light puts you back into your power and makes you a stronger magnet for miracles and magical opportunities.

🕐 10–30 minutes or more

1. Find a comfortable, seated position, close your eyes, and begin allowing your breath to tune you into your energy and being.

2. Bring your awareness to the column of light emanating from all your energy centers in sync. Your crown (top of head), third eye (brow point), throat, heart, solar plexus, sacral center (six inches below your navel), and root (where you are seated) are all lit up with bright white light, forming a dazzling column. Breathe into this awareness and light for a few minutes.

3. Now see all those same energy centers with an additional beam of light going directly in front of them and behind them: one column of light from the top of your head to the bottom of your tailbone, and another going out six feet from your front and back. Breathe here, resting your awareness in this light for a few minutes.

4. Next, each energy center radiates another column of light, this time going out six feet from both the right and left sides of your body. Breathe into the awareness of all three of these light columns coming out of your being. Stay here for several minutes, remembering, with each breath, that *you are light.*

5. Feel the love, joy, acceptance, compassion, and potential in all this light of yours. Sit in it for a few minutes before gently opening your eyes and sharing that light with the world.

19. Remembering Oneness

We're all made of the same divine source. We all have souls that just want us to experience joy, love, and acceptance. However, as we go through our days, it's easy for us to give our power away by elevating someone in our estimation above others, withholding forgiveness, or falling into judgment. This meditation brings us back to our truth so that we take our power back and treat everyone in our life as an equal.

🕐 **10–30 minutes or more**

1. Begin in a seated position with your spine straight and your eyes closed. Let your breath assist you in relaxing and bringing your awareness inside.

2. Bring your awareness to your heart, your soul, the very core essence of your being. See it as a sparkling ball of golden light, growing larger with each breath.

3. Envision someone you love dearly in front of you. See them sitting there face-to-face with you. Notice the very same ball of light in their heart center, glowing and expanding as they breathe. They, too, just want to be happy, dancing between their human and their infinite nature. They're doing the best they can right now. Take a couple of minutes to really take this in and observe them. Feel the love you have for them as one with you.

4. Next, envision someone you have a harder time liking. Invite them to sit in front of you. Notice that same ball of golden light at the core of their being. See them as another infinite being having a human experience, simply wanting to be happy and loved. Take a couple of minutes here to truly open up to seeing this.

5. Last, imagine a busy pedestrian street in your neighborhood, full of people walking. See them all, each with their own golden balls of light at the core of their being—all doing their best to be happy, feel loved, and navigate this dance between their human and their divine selves.

6. Feel the love and the connection you feel for all these people. Remind yourself that we're all made up of the same essence. We all strive for joy, love, and acceptance, and we're all navigating the journey as best we can.

20. Connecting to Your Infinite Potential

At our purest essence, we're infinite, and we have infinite potentials in the universe—but most of us don't walk around feeling anywhere close to that. This meditation gives us some much-needed help to tap back into our potential and all the possibilities within.

🕐 10–30 minutes or more

1. Sit comfortably and close your eyes. Allow your breath to draw your attention inward and begin shifting your awareness from anything outside you.

2. Bring your focus to your heart center. Breathe into this area, and allow the rest of your physical body to melt away until you feel as if you're a floating heart space.

3. Notice the infinite space around you—infinite space above, below, and on each side. Become aware that you're simply an essence in an unlimited universe. Stay here, deepening this awareness for a few minutes.

4. You're now in the quantum field, a space full of potential and possibilities. In this creation space, you can select any frequency in the field that matches your desired next evolution, and call it toward you. What are you calling forth? Feel its frequency integrating with your awareness in the field. Stay here for a few minutes.

5. Come back into your body, and allow this new frequency to activate in every particle of your being. Feel your whole being shifting to accommodate it. Take in the feeling of its already being your reality. Spend a few minutes here to fully embody it.

6. Close with a few deep breaths of gratitude and continue your day, owning the new frequency you've selected for your life.

Meditations to Activate Your Heart's Desires

So many of us bury our heart's desires because they don't feel practical anymore, and we wouldn't know how to even start pursuing them. Or maybe we've gotten so caught up in just getting through our day-to-day that we barely consider them. Activating your heart's desire is like turning on your manifesting GPS. It shows you the direction your soul was meant to take. In the meditations in this section, you'll become intimate with your deepest desires. You'll gain clarity on what the dream life looks like, therefore turning up your magnetism to attract it into your reality.

21. Talking to Your Heart

Our heart space is the center for our truest self. It's where our individual truth lives, and it's also where our higher truth lives. It's from this sacred place that we uncover the desires or vision for our lives that will bring us true joy and fulfillment.

🕐 10–30 minutes or more

1. Sit in a comfortable position, place your hands on your heart, close your eyes, and begin taking deep breaths in and out of your heart center.

2. Allow your breath to connect you deeper into your heart. Feel your heart opening up and communicating with your entire being, each cell receiving a message of love, truth, and gratitude from your heart.

3. Silently, ask your heart, "What do you deeply desire?" Give it some space to speak by simple breathing and being open to receiving. Notice what arises—thoughts, feelings, visions, and so on. Sit here for a few minutes while the answers come forward.

4. Connect your awareness in your heart to your awareness in your third eye (between and above your eyebrows). Ask your heart to show you the vision it has for your most soul-aligned life. Sit here for several minutes until the answers come forward.

5. When you feel complete, take a deep breath in through your nose and out through your mouth, filling yourself up with so much gratitude for all that you have received.

22. Your Childhood Dreams

When we were kids, we dreamed big—no one tried to make us more realistic. Instead, we were encouraged to role-play our dreams with make-believe kitchen sets, firefighter trucks, or dress-up doctor outfits and plastic stethoscopes. Our urges to explore the variety of ways we could express ourselves in the world were encouraged. Going back to this time allows us to open up to the endless possibilities for our work in the world.

🕐 10–30 minutes or more

1. Begin by sitting or lying in a comfortable position with your eyes closed. Start breathing deeply and relaxing into your body. Allow your breath to release any tension you've been holding on to.

2. Bring your awareness to the core of your being, envisioning a ball of golden light there. Breathe in and out of this ball of light, watching it expand and glow more and more brightly as your awareness of your physical world and physical body melts away.

3. Next, call on your childhood self, at whatever age they appear. Trust that exactly the version of you that you need will show up. See them standing in front of you with so much love.

4. Ask them, "What do you dream of being when you grow up?" "What do you want your adult life to look like?" "Is there anything you want to tell me or remind me of?" Allow yourself to sit in this conversation for several minutes.

5. Feel your childhood self hug you for listening and truly hearing them. Then bring your awareness back into your body. Close your practice with a few deep breaths of gratitude for this experience.

23. Your Best Day Ever

This meditation can be used in one of two ways. You can either imagine your best day ever, where you're living the life your heart most desires, or you can imagine *today* being the best version of it ever. Preplanning your day in the creative space allows you to use your manifestation power to steer your day or to call in that future best day ever by anchoring yourself in the experience.

🕐 10–30 minutes or more

1. Sit in a supportive position with your back straight and your body relaxed. Place your palms in your lap, facing up. Close your eyes, and roll them up to your third eye (the spot between and a bit above your eyebrows). Start taking some long, deep breaths.

2. Continue to breathe, with your awareness at your third eye. Choose whether you'll visualize your best day ever, or the best version of the day ahead of you. Begin to allow the thoughts of what would be included in that day to gently pop into your awareness.

3. When you're ready, begin visualizing this ideal day from the moment you wake up in the morning until you go to sleep that night. Notice all the details—your feelings during the day and the events that make it even more amazing. Savor and soak up your experience as you watch yourself move through this day.

4. Once you feel complete and conclude your best day ever, allow yourself to bask in the gratitude you have for the day you just experienced for a few minutes. Just breathe and feel how thankful you are in your heart.

5. When you're ready to close, take a deep breath in, hold it, lock in this gratitude, and exhale. Now bring the energy of that day into the rest of yours!

24. Wishes Fulfilled

For this meditation, we'll use a Jupiter mudra (hand gesture) to activate the planet of good luck and blessings. We'll continue to activate our desires by tapping into "our magic wand" and claiming all our wishes fulfilled.

🕐 **10–30 minutes or more**

1. Begin by finding a comfortable, supported, seated position. Place your fingers in Jupiter mudra by interlacing all your fingers except your two index fingers—think of making a pretend gun with your hands, as if for *Charlie's Angels*-type photos. Place your wrists at your heart center so your index fingers are angled slightly up. Imagine this as the wand that will make your wishes come true.

2. Close your eyes and take some deep breaths to bring your awareness inward and release anything that's going on around you.

3. Breathe into your heart center, activating the mudra. Feel into the possibility of wishes fulfilled. What would it be like to simply be able to grant your own wishes?

4. Allow your mind to intentionally wander to all the wishes you would grant yourself and others. Where would you wave your wand? What would you use your power for? Let whatever arises arise! Maybe you're waving your wand to give a little kid an ice cream cone, or to land your dream job, or for your parents' perfect health. Be playful and push the limits of what you would do.

5. When you feel complete, bring your awareness back into your breath and your heart center. Feel how powerful you are. Feel the joy of being a creator and of the places where your energy can make an impact. Integrate it all, and notice how this experience has raised your energy and vibration level. Unlace your hands, hold them up above your head, and take a deep breath in. Hold it, locking in all this energy, and then exhale.

25. Your Divine Vision

Cultivating a divine vision is an important part of the manifesting process. Think of it as how we aim our arrow before we let it fly. This is a meditation from my Divinely Design Your Life program. It will allow you not only to see your vision but also to break it down into three different layers, as we noted in part I, for more effective manifestation.

🕐 10–30 minutes or more

1. Find yourself a supported position where you can fully relax your body (as long as you won't fall asleep!). Close your eyes, and begin slowing down your breath. Allow your mind to wander around what might be 1 to 5 years down the line for you if you truly become a powerful creator of your reality.

2. Let your breath become deeper, your body even more relaxed. Surrender to the cushion or floor beneath you, and allow your consciousness to become detached from your surroundings.

3. Let yourself float into your divine vision for the next level of your life. What does your world look like? How do you feel as you go through your day? What goals have you accomplished? Just observe and expand your vision so that experiencing it lights you up. It's your dream life. Linger here for several minutes.

4. When you feel that you've fully locked it in, bring your awareness back to your heart. Fill yourself with so much gratitude for this experience on its way to you.

5. As you gently open your eyes and come back into the room, grab a journal and a writing utensil. Jot down answers to these questions:

   - What were the overall feelings I had about my life in this vision? How can I bring them into my life right now?
   - What goals had I accomplished in this vision? Am I taking aligned action toward them each day? What might that look like?
   - What was the genuine essence behind this vision or this new level of life? Is there something I can do to bring that into my life now?

26. Surrendering to Your Soul's Desires (Bath Meditation)

It's easy for us to get caught up in our day-to-day life, stuck on a trajectory dictated by the world around us, not by our soul's desires. This bath-time meditation allows you a space to truly let the stress of the outside world dissipate. Relax and go deep within to hear what your soul is craving.

🕐 10–30 minutes or more

1. Run yourself a bath at an ideal temperature for you. Feel free to add Epsom salts, essential oils, or something else to make it even more delightful. (My go-to is usually lavender Epsom salt with rose and ylang-ylang essential oils, and I light a few candles.)

2. Find a comfortable, supported position in the bath so you can relax without your head sinking under water. Close your eyes, and allow your breath to assist your body in relaxing further.

3. Feel the warm, nourishing waters around you. Imagine that you're bathing in the waters of all the possibilities for your life. They are floating around you—all your desires, big and small. Just observe them, without judgment and without thinking. Notice what desires and potentials are floating around. Do this for a few minutes.

4. Set the intention for the most important desires to rise to the top of your mind. Keep yourself open, and be willing to receive them no matter what they might be. Notice what arises.

5. Feel the feelings of all these desires coming true. Allow yourself to fantasize about all the ways they could show up in your life and how they would feel when they arrive.

6. When you're finished and feeling lit up from all your soul's desires, open your eyes and enjoy the rest of your bath.

27. Living the Daydream (Walking Meditation)

This is a truly playful and mood-lifting active meditation that will give you the chance to break the glass ceiling around your desires and step into just how well things could turn out. This meditation is a powerful energetic pull for your manifestations to come to life.

🕐 15–30 minutes or more

1. Arrive at the park or walking path where you'll do your walking meditation. Stand up straight, put your hands on your heart, and close your eyes. Gently begin breathing into your heart center, activating and expanding it.

2. Once you feel grounded in your heart, allow all the exciting and joyful desires you're ready to bring into reality to start bubbling up to the surface from your heart. Stand for another minute or two, just observing all that floats up to your awareness.

3. Open your eyes. Feel free to turn on some music that pumps you up (visit cassandrabodzak.com/manifesting for playlist ideas). Begin walking like the powerful creator you are, with your eyes lightly focused on the horizon.

4. As you walk, release your hands down to your sides and allow yourself to daydream about all the different magical and surprising ways your desire could arrive. Maybe it will come through a friend of a friend, or take the form of a random email on a Tuesday. Perhaps someone will mention your name to the right person. Maybe you'll win a contest or bump into someone at the coffee shop who can help you. The possibilities are endless. Allow yourself to get lost in all the possibilities. You're expanding the potentials of your own belief system while doing this very fun work. Keep going for the next 15 to 20 minutes, completely enjoying the experience of each new idea.

5. When you're complete, come back to standing still with your hands on your heart. Take a few closing breaths in with gratitude for all that is on its way to you.

28. Planting the Seed

Manifesting our desires is a lot like planting seeds in a garden. Our desire is the seed: When we plant it in the ground, we're setting the intention for it to grow, and we're giving it to the universe or source. We "water" our desires by feeling the feelings of them already here, we give them sunshine by believing they're on their way, and we protect them by releasing our fears and negative beliefs around their coming to fruition.

🕐 10–30 minutes or more

1. Sit in a comfortable, seated position with your spine elongated and your eyes closed. Begin taking some deep breaths to relax the body and tune inward.

2. Allow any thoughts that may come up to pass by like clouds, gently bringing your attention back to your breath. Clear your mind and allow yourself to melt away from your physical reality, feeling as if you were simply your breath. Give yourself a few minutes to get here.

3. Visualize yourself sitting next to a nice plot of soil. You have a handful of seeds to your right and a small shovel to your left. Pick up one seed at a time. Hold it in your hand and infuse it with the energy of something you'd like to manifest in your life. Then pick up the shovel, dig a little hole, and plant that seed with intention. As you cover it up with soil, place both your hands on the seed and see what its blossoming would look like. Repeat with all the desires you wish to plant right now.

4. Take a deep breath as you look at all the beautiful desires you've planted in your plot. Envision what your life will look like once they all blossom. Sit with that vision, and soak it in.

5. Ask your highest self, "What do I need to water these seeds? How can I make sure they get the sunshine they need to grow?" Listen to whatever comes up, and spend a few minutes here.

6. When you're complete, take a deep breath in, with excitement for all that is blossoming in your life, and exhale with trust.

29. New Moon Intention Setting

New moon is a powerful time to set intentions and start manifesting a desire in alignment with the astrological energies. A new moon is a time when we will naturally be drawn to setting new goals, beginning new projects or a new relationship, and a time to honor what's naturally arising for us. This meditation works for any new moon. Use it as a go-to baseline to ride this cosmic wave of energy!

1. To start, gather a piece of paper, a pencil or pen, a candle in a glass jar, and any crystals, herbs, or essential oils you feel called to play with for this particular moon. Trust your intuition when selecting! If you don't have any of the extras, you can still do this with paper, pen, and candle.

2. Set up your space the way you want it. On the piece of paper, write what you're manifesting for this new moon in the present tense— for example, "I have an amazing job that pays me abundantly for my good work." Fold it up and place it under your glass jar candle.

3. Take a moment to sit with the energy of that manifestation, then light the candle as you invite the universe, your higher self, and any divine support you'd like to assist you in manifesting this intention.

4. Once the candle is lit, close your eyes, and feel energy of the moon pouring down light into your crown, your third eye, your throat, your heart, your solar plexus, your sacral area, and your root—activating this manifestation in every energy center. Allow yourself to receive this light, and let it flow through your being several times. Each time, feel how supported your manifestation is. Acknowledge how amazing it will feel and your deep trust that it's on its way.

5. When you're complete, take a deep breath in and hold it, locking in the lunar support of your manifestation, and exhale. Keep the candle lit until it burns out fully (in a safe place!), and then recycle both the jar and the paper. It's done!

30. Connecting to the Essence of Your Desire

In part I, we talked about getting down to the essence of your desire, a concept that is likely new to many of you. This meditation will assist you in peeling back the layers covering your desires to get clarity on the core essence behind those layers. When we have clarity around the core essence, we can bring that into our life now and expedite our manifestation.

🕐 **10–30 minutes or more**

1. Find a comfortable, supportive position and close your eyes. Relax your body and allow your breath to help you center into this moment.

2. Bring your awareness to your heart center. With every inhale and exhale, allow your external reality to melt away, and begin to rest in your heart. Take as long as you need to get here.

3. Once you're in your heart, bring up your desire, or whatever you're trying to manifest currently. Allow yourself to see it fully—feel your desire for it, and feel the excitement of it being on its way.

4. Now go even deeper, and ask your heart's consciousness, "What is this desire really all about at its core?" "What do I truly want to feel or experience in the manifesting of this?" "Are there any specifics or details that I can release to get this desire to its purest form?" "Are there aspects of how this desire comes about that I can release to get down to the real desire?" Spend several minutes here. Allow the layers to peel away as you get closer to the pure essence of your desire. Once you find it, rest there for a moment.

5. To close, bring your hands to your heart. Take a deep breath in and out, with gratitude for the clarity you have received.

Meditations to Release Fear and Limitations

Releasing the beliefs, fears, and preconceived limitations that we have around anything we want to manifest is often the most critical step to manifesting. So much of what blocks us is that deep down in our subconscious, we don't actually believe we can have or attract that thing into our lives. This will cut off your manifestation every time. These meditations give you the tools to chop down those fears from all different angles and clear the pathway for your vision to become a reality.

31. Exhaling Fear and Inhaling Trust

Sometimes the most effective way to shift our vibration to a more magnetic frequency is to keep it general. Using the words *fear* and *trust* releases our attachment to whatever specific story of limitation we may be navigating, allowing us to get back to the essence of what we need to do: release fear and embody trust. This meditation can be used for any trigger, fear, or worry in the way of your manifestation, and it can be done virtually anywhere—even with your eyes open!

🕐 20–30 minutes or more

1. If you're at home, get into a comfortable position and close your eyes. If you're at work, driving, or walking around, simply take a few breaths to prepare your body for the meditation. Keep your eyes open, in light focus on whatever is in front of you.

2. Set the intention for releasing any and all fears, known and unknown, around whatever desire you're manifesting, or even the dream vision of your life in general.

3. On each inhale, breathe in trust. Trust that it's on its way. Trust that the universe/source/the divine is supporting and assisting you always. Trust that you're a powerful creator. Trust that your desire is part of your inevitable future. Feel the feelings of this trust in your body every time you inhale.

4. On each exhale, release any and all fears standing in your way. Let go from every particle of your being, remove them from your DNA and personal memories, and release any fear, limitation, or belief that is not in your highest good. On each exhale, feel your body release more and more on the conscious and unconscious levels.

5. Continue with this inhale-exhale pattern for another 10 to 20 minutes, or until you feel fully trusting and empty of fears (if that comes sooner).

6. Take a deep breath to lock it in. Hold your breath, and feel trust permeating every cell of your being. Feel excitement for your manifestation on its way. Exhale, and if you closed your eyes, open them.

32. Divine Truth Test

When you start looking at the fears getting in your way, it's important to take them through a "divine truth check." Often, we build up evidence for our fear based on our own earthly, limited thinking, and we need to surrender it to the divine to see it clearly. When we do this, we manifest a miracle—we shift our fear-based thinking to a love-centered truth and open the path to divine creation!

🕐 10–30 minutes or more

1. Take a look at your fear inventory, or pick a fear or limiting belief that's rearing its ugly head for you today. This will be the subject of our divine truth test. When you're ready, get into a comfortable position for the meditation.

2. Close your eyes, and start taking some longer breaths from your heart space. Allow yourself to sit with this fear statement while breathing in and out, expanding the light in your heart center.

3. Call in any divine help you'd like to assist in this process. This can be your highest self, the universe, the source, the divine of your design, angels, passed-on loved ones, or even love consciousness itself. Invite whichever higher beings resonate with you deeply. Feel a cord of light connecting your heart to their energy as you welcome them into the space.

4. Energetically place your fear statement before you, as if setting it down on a table or altar before your higher counsel for review. Ask them to show you the higher truth of this statement, and allow yourself to open your mind and your heart to receiving.

5. Feel light energy flowing from them through your heart cord into you as they send you messages, visions, and feelings about the real truth of the matter. Feel the statement now held in divine truth of your infinite abundance, limitless possibilities, and the powerful, divine creator you are. Stay here as long as needed to receive this truth.

6. When you're ready, ask them for a divine truth statement— something that you can now implant within your consciousness to take the place of this fear or limited belief. Thank them for their wisdom and perspective.

7. Come back into your heart and into the room. Sit with your new, true statement for a minute before opening your eyes and going into the day. Write down the new statement to help you remember to replace your old fear statement with the divine truth. If the old fear pops up again, you'll have its replacement.

33. Reparenting Meditation

In my manifesting master's program, Divinely Design Your Life, we tackle what I call "the root wounds." These come from events in our childhood that caused us to believe certain things about ourselves or about life, and they can be the most insidious of perpetrators. Perhaps our parents passed on to us their own limiting beliefs. Luckily, we can return to the moment we first learned the belief that's blocking us, and reparent ourselves from our present knowledge, shifting this pattern in our energetic field for good. That's what this meditation is all about.

🕐 10–30 minutes or more

1. Start by choosing the fear or limiting belief that you want to work with for today's meditation. Ask yourself, "When was the first time I remember believing this?" "How old was I when I first started believing this?" "What was the event that made me take this on as truth?" It doesn't have to be perfect, and don't worry about finding the absolute earliest event—just trust whatever memory boils up to the top of your consciousness first, and go with it.

2. Close your eyes, and allow your breath to help you go deep within to the quiet, loving space at the center of your being. When you're there, bring up the memory you're working with today.

3. Observe your childhood self. Watch them as the scene plays out. What are they doing? What meanings did they make out of it? How did it shape them? Now pull your view of the situation back to see it as your highest self. What was really going on? What were the adults in the situation doing? What in their behaviors was being influenced by their limited thinking or beliefs? Give yourself several minutes to truly see this memory, with all the factors involved, from a higher perspective.

4. Now see your highest self going into this memory to comfort your youngest self as a parent with a loving, abundant consciousness would. Hug your younger self. Let them know how loved and how amazing they are. Explain to them anything about the situation that would allow them to make a different meaning from it. Let them ask you any questions until they feel at peace with this new positive belief about what happened, or in spite of what happened.

5. When you feel complete, give your younger self one last hug. Let them know that you're always here for them, that they're never alone, and that you love them very much.

6. Bring your awareness back to your heart center. Take a few deep breaths to integrate the healing into every particle of your being. When you're ready, gently open your eyes and stretch your body in any way that feels nourishing. Feel free to journal on any new ah-has or beliefs that you'd like to solidify further.

34. Full Moon Meditation

Full moons are the astrological moment of releasing or letting go. Fun fact: They can also be a time when the manifestations you set on a new moon come to fruition! However, for this meditation, we'll focus on the cosmic support we have at this time to deeply release behaviors, patterns, fears, or beliefs that are blocking us from living the life we crave. You can do this meditation in your usual nook, or try it in a lovely bath with Epsom salts and essential oils if you feel called—either works fabulously!

🕐 10–30 minutes or more

1. Take a deep breath in as you close your eyes and find a comfortable, supported position. Let your inhales and exhales ground and center you more deeply into your being, allowing the rest of the world to fall away.

2. Spend a few minutes here, resting in the spacious nothingness of your breath in the safe darkness of your very self. Let thoughts pass by as you continue to go more deeply into this infinite space. Take as long as you need to arrive here.

3. From this place, see yourself sitting at the end of a dock on a beautiful lake. To your right is a pile of rocks, which represent the habits, patterns, or limiting beliefs that you're ready to release on this full moon.

4. Grab one rock at a time, feel its weight in your hand, and see the behavior or belief associated with it. Transfer its energy from your being to the rock. When you're ready, powerfully throw that rock into the lake. Watch the ripples as the lake takes the weight of the rock from you. Allow yourself a moment to feel the lightness of the release.

5. Repeat for as many rocks and releases as you have right now.

6. When you're complete, place your hands on your heart. Bow your head in gratitude to the lake, to the moon, and to the universe for taking this negative energy from you. When you open your eyes, trust that it is released, and move forward accordingly.

35. Releasing Anxiety

Ah, anxiety. Who doesn't dance with it these days? And yet anxiety can be such a roadblock for us when it comes to stepping into our next-level life. Why? Because when we're racked by anxiety, we have forgotten that we are a divine creator of our life. This meditation will help relieve and release your anxious feelings so that you can remember who you are and get back to magnetizing toward you the life you dream of.

1. Sit or lie down, finding a comfortable position in which to fully relax. Close your eyes, and begin focusing on your breath—in through your nose, out through your mouth. Allow your breath alone to soothe you and calm your nervous system.

2. Locate where anxiety is living in your body. It may be in one spot or a few different spots. Notice where it is, and breathe into that/those area(s).

3. Give your anxiety a shape and a color. What shape does anxiety take in your body? What color comes to mind when you tap into it?

4. Now see that shape in its color illuminated. Feel it rise out of your body, rising all the way to the ceiling in the room, through the roof of your home, up into the sky, and dissipating into the galaxy. Repeat for as many areas of anxiety as you have.

5. Come back into your body, and breathe pure white light into the space the anxiety has just vacated, infusing with it the knowledge of your truth and your innate creative power.

6. Take a few more deep breaths, noticing how your energy feels now. Feel thankful for your ability to remove anxiety from your being.

36. Surrendering to Feeling the Fear

A powerful exercise in learning to move through your fear—or "feel the fear and do it anyway," as they say—is being able to sit in the fear you have. This short meditation will make you slightly uncomfortable at first, but then ultimately it will give you back your power over your fears. It's a game changer!

1. Assume a seated position with your back straight and your body relaxed. Begin taking some nourishing breaths in through your nose and out through your mouth.

2. Bring the situation regarding the fear you're facing today to the top of your mind. Notice how this fear is stopping you from taking aligned action with your desires, causing you distress, and blocking your manifestation.

3. Ask yourself, "What's my worst-case scenario? What am I so afraid of?"

4. Whatever arises, sit in the feeling of it having happened for 60 to 90 seconds. Allow yourself to feel all the feelings associated with this fear-come-true, but maintain your breathing as you sit in the experience.

5. When you're complete, release it, shake it off, and come back to your heart and your breath. How does it feel to know that you can withstand the worst-case scenario? Feel the unlikeliness of it happening in your body, but also the confidence of knowing you could handle it.

6. Ask yourself, "Am I willing to feel the fear and choose my dreams anyway?" Reflect and then journal on this experience once you open your eyes.

37. Meeting Your Inner Saboteur

As we progress on our manifestation journey, one thing remains the same: Our biggest saboteur will always be ourselves. In this meditation, we'll observe the different ways we sabotage our creations from a higher perspective, so that we can call ourselves out and break the cycle.

1. Find a relaxed position, seated or lying down. Close your eyes, and begin tuning into your inner world through your breath. Allow the awareness of your external reality to fade away as your awareness centers simply on your breath.

2. Feel your awareness floating up above your body. Your awareness rises even farther until it is on the ceiling of the room you're in, looking down at you meditating.

3. From this vantage point, your awareness will witness what being a "fly on the wall" for a few days of your life feels like. Watch yourself as you move through the past week. Notice the behaviors, habits, or thought patterns that drag you down or stop you in your tracks.

4. Set the intention to witness your saboteur. Where do you procrastinate? Where do you distract yourself? Where do you give away your power? Where do you go into negative thought spirals? Are there ways that you dull your greatness or compromise yourself to people-please? Sit here for at least 10 minutes, and soak it all in.

5. When you're complete, bring your awareness back down into your body, focusing on your breath. Sit here, now powerfully aware of how to stop your own sabotage.

6. Grab your journal and write down everything that came up about the ways you sabotage yourself. Bringing this to your consciousness will naturally help you put an end to it as soon as it starts to creep up again.

38. Washing Away Fear (Shower Meditation)

This shower meditation is something I do every time I rinse off. It's a super-easy, highly effective way to intentionally release fear and limitations on a regular basis. Let your shower do double duty—not just cleansing the dirt off your body but also washing away the fears in your mind.

🕐 **10–30 minutes or more**

1. Set your intention before you get into the shower. Is there a specific fear, limiting belief, or self-sabotaging pattern that is coming up for you today that you'd like to intentionally release? Or would you like to do a more general release of anything that may be getting in the way of your desire coming into form? Either is perfect, or feel free to alternate, depending on how you are feeling.

2. Once you're in the shower, with the water running down your body and your body wash (or however you clean yourself) going, feel the water and the soap literally scrubbing out the fear, limiting beliefs, or self-sabotaging patterns from your being.

3. As you become cleaner, more water washes away the dirt, along with what you're releasing. Feel yourself returning to the truth of who you are as an infinitely abundant being—full of love, boundlessly supported, with limitless possibilities and potential.

4. Finish your shower and dry off as you allow a smile to come to your face in acknowledgment of your return to your truth.

39. Walking Out of Your Past (Walking Meditation)

Our past is quite literally behind us, and when we linger there we find ourselves sitting so often in helplessness, disempowerment, or struggle. It's no surprise we would feel that way because our power is in the present. With this walking meditation, you'll leave your past behind you and step into your creative power in the present moment. This is an especially potent meditation for when you're in a funk and want to move out of it.

🕐 **10–30 minutes or more**

1. Find a path or trail for practicing your walking meditation. Begin by standing still, closing your eyes, and breathing into your heart space.

2. Ask yourself, "What is it from my past I am walking out of today?" "What is in my highest good to finally step forward from and leave behind?" Trust whatever arises.

3. When you have it, gently open your eyes, and fix them on the horizon in soft focus. Begin imagining yourself walking out of past memories, events, or beliefs that you're leaving behind. Feel free to play music during this walk if it helps. A powerful drumbeat or tribal track can work wonders for activating a bit more energy in your walk.

4. See the memories, the situations that played out, the old ways you had been behaving or reacting, the way that certain beliefs held you back or that patterns kept you stuck. See it all as you walk forward, moving past it, leaving it in your dust.

5. Once you feel that you've walked fully out of your past, begin to acknowledge this present moment and all its potential. See yourself walking into all the miraculous potentials for your life—all the amazing things that could happen for you, all the ways you show up as your best self in this present moment, the beliefs that your present self is committed to believing, etc.

6. When you're ready to close your walk, stand still once again. Place your hands on your heart, and take several breaths in gratitude for standing in your present moment, with all its power and potential.

40. Shaking Off Negative Thoughts

Ever seen a dog shake their whole body? My little Yorkie does it all the time. It's actually how they release stress and recalibrate their nervous systems. Carl, my dog, has a lot of anxiety, so he loves to shake it out. One day, I figured I'd give it a whirl, too. Lo and behold, shaking it out is also extraordinarily helpful for us humans! If you're feeling anxious, stressed, or angry, or you're just experiencing a lot of negative thoughts, this active meditation will become a fast friend!

🕐 10–30 minutes or more

1. Sit or stand up, depending on whether you want to use your whole body or just the upper half. Either works great! If you'd like to play a favorite upbeat song to complement the meditation, start that now. Personally, I love to use Florence + the Machine's "Shake It Out" while doing this practice, but music is not necessary.

2. Close your eyes, raise your arms above your head as if you were holding a great big pasteboard sign at a concert, and begin shaking your entire being! Shake, shake, shake it out. Keep your hands up and shake the entire time.

3. Feel yourself releasing all those negative thoughts, all those limiting beliefs, any block getting in your way as you continue to shake, breathing freely and powerfully. Allow the energy you release to excavate all your negative thoughts from your mind and any other particle of your being where they may be stored.

4. Continue for about 3 minutes, or until the song you chose ends.

5. Release your arms down to your sides and place your palms, facing up, on your knees. If you were standing, now is a good time to sit or lie down. Allow your breath to connect to your heart center as you bask in the feelings of this release.

6. Feel the spaciousness you created in your being. Feel your nervous system rebalancing, and breathe into your heart's truth for another few minutes. Fully enjoy this state before bringing your hands to your heart center and bowing your head down in gratitude to yourself for showing up today and doing the work.

Meditations to Embody the Future You

As we discussed in part I, the third step of manifestation is embodiment. We need to feel as if we already have what we're calling in. We need to become the next-level version of ourselves now, bringing in the next level of opportunities or circumstances from that place. These meditations will give you 10 different ways to do just that. Enjoy the new you!

41. Meeting You 2.0

We can't separate the 2.0 version of our life from the 2.0 version of ourselves—they go hand in hand. Each new evolution of our life, each new fulfillment of our desires, will give birth to a new version of ourselves. In this meditation, we'll make contact with that 2.0 version of us that already has everything we're manifesting, and see what guidance they have for us.

🕐 10–30 minutes or more

1. Get into a comfortable, seated or lying-down position. Close your eyes and roll them upward, toward your third eye (just above and between your eyebrows). Begin breathing in through your nose and out through your mouth. Allow your body to relax.

2. Keep your awareness on your third eye as you allow your breath to release any stress or tension in your body. Let the world drift away as you simply focus on each inhale and exhale, and your third eye.

3. Visualize your 2.0 self through your third eye. This is the version of you that is already living the life of your dreams. See it projected before you, as if on a movie screen. What do they look like? What clothes are they wearing? What energy do they give off? What habits do they have? What kinds of things are they up to?

4. When you have fully taken in you 2.0, ask them to come in closer so you can speak with them. Ask them what guidance they have for you. What advice do they want to tell you about the journey you're on? Are there action steps, habits, or feelings that you can embrace right now?

5. When you feel complete, thank them for sharing their wisdom. Bring your breath back to your third eye and back into your body. When you're ready, open your eyes.

42. Embodying Future You

This next meditation builds on the last one. We'll take it one step further and merge with our future selves to fully embody them in the now. This is a process I like to call "quantum embodiment" in my Divinely Design Your Life curriculum, and it's a very powerful part of successful manifesting.

🕐 10–30 minutes or more

1. Get into a comfortable, seated position in a room where you'll have at least a small amount of space to stand and move around. Close your eyes, and turn them up to your third eye. Use your breath to relax the body and release any tension.

2. Take a few minutes to completely unwind your body, clear your mind, and release the outside world.

3. When you're ready, see the future you (or you 2.0) in front of you. Observe them—how they hold themselves, the energy they exude. Take in all of it.

4. Gently stand up so you're standing face-to-face with future you. Watch them as they move forward, eventually meshing with your body and integrating into you.

5. Feel yourself upgrading on the cellular level as you integrate this future version of you into your current operating system. Notice how your posture changes, how your energy shifts, how your thoughts elevate, and more. Take several minutes to allow this full process to run its course and for you to fully embody the future you.

6. Slowly walk around the room as your future you (walking in circles is fine). You can open your eyes just a little bit so you don't bump into anything. Walk as this future you that you've just integrated. See how this changes your movement, your feelings, and beyond.

7. When you're complete, open your eyes fully and continue on with your day as your future you—except now, it's just you!

43. Walking into the Future (Walking Meditation)

Now that you're getting better and better at embodying the next-level version of you, let's take it a step further: Bring that version of you into the real world with a walking meditation. This meditation is a great bridge from the quantum embodiment work you do in your meditation to showing up that way as you go about your daily life.

🕐 20–30 minutes or more

1. Find a good path or track that you can walk on safely. If you want, bring a playlist of songs to listen to that are uplifting or that align with your future you. Stand still for a few minutes. Close your eyes, and breathe into your heart space and your third eye at once, activating them both.

2. When you feel connected to your heart and third eye, welcome the energy of your future self into your being. Feel your energy and body shift into the next-level you who is ready to step up—the you where your dreams are already your reality.

3. Once you've got it locked in, open your eyes to a soft focus on the horizon in front of you. Begin walking powerfully as your future self. Play upbeat or inspiring music that helps get you in the zone (this is optional).

4. As you're walking as your next-level you, imagine all the events, meetings, and situations you're walking into. Experience the excitement, gratitude, and power you feel for this new evolution. Continue walking and embodying this energy for another 10 to 20 minutes.

5. When you feel complete, stand still. Place your hands on your heart, and put a big smile on your face. Feel the immense gratitude you have for the you you're stepping into.

44. Upgrading Your Mind

To shift the way we are in the world, we first need to shift the way we are in our heads. Our thoughts create our reality and our experience of the world. If you're ready to embody your future self, you need to upgrade your mind to think the thoughts of your future self. That's exactly what this meditation is for.

🕐 20–30 minutes or more

1. Get into a comfortable, seated position. Close your eyes, and begin breathing in through your nose and out through your mouth. Allow your shoulders to melt down and your body to relax.

2. Notice whatever thoughts are coming up, and gently let them pass by as you continue to bring yourself back to your breath and become the observer of each thought.

3. Ask yourself as the thoughts come up, "Would my future self think this?" If not, replace it. For example, you think, "I need to get to my to-do list. I'm so overwhelmed." Your future self may instead choose the thought, "I have plenty of time to get everything accomplished today that I need to." Maybe a thought comes up about

your dream life: "I have no idea how I will get that promotion." Ask yourself what the you who is already living your dream life would think about the same thing.

4. Continue with this reprogramming of your thoughts, one thought at a time, for 10 to 20 minutes. This will create profound shifts each time you do this meditation. Don't worry if the same type of thought keeps coming up during a session—this is just showing you what needs some extra love to shift!

5. Spend a few minutes just thinking the thoughts of your future self. Marinate in the optimism, the possibility, the confidence, and the excitement of this mind-set.

6. When you're complete, bring your awareness back into your breath and your body. Slowly stretch, moving in whatever way feels good, and open your eyes. Pay attention to that future you who is now in the back of your head throughout the day, and continue to flip any outdated thoughts on the spot!

45. Timeline Hopping

We're all on a certain trajectory, or timeline, for our lives right now, one that is based on our current beliefs, energy, and aligned action-taking. When we shift our trajectory, we're elevating to a new level of self-belief, creative energy, and greater flow of aligned action-taking. This is what helps us shift the course of our life in a profound way, and this is what we'll anchor in through this meditation.

🕐 10–30 minutes or more

1. Get into a comfortable position where you can completely relax your body. Close your eyes, and begin to focus on your breath. Let any thoughts that arise float by as you refocus on your breath and surrender any tension.

2. Bring your awareness to the core of your being, your navel center. Envision a golden ball of light there, expanding with each breath. Let this ball of light grow until it encompasses your entire being, and you become one with it.

3. As your physical being melts away and you surrender to your light body, set the intention to witness the timeline or trajectory you're currently on, based on your beliefs, energy, and actions up to this moment.

4. Next, energetically intend to move to a higher timeline or trajectory that is directly aligned with the highest vision you have for your life. See the beliefs, energy, and actions associated with this timeline.

5. Consciously allow the beliefs, energy, and inspiration for action of this new timeline to meld into your subconscious and all the particles of your being. Sit here until you feel that this process is complete. Be patient and let it soak in.

6. When you're ready, bring your awareness back into your body, breathing life into this new timeline. Open your eyes, and act in accordance with the new beliefs, energy, and inspired aligned action-taking you've chosen to step into. Return to this meditation whenever you feel yourself drifting back into the old timeline.

46. Watching Your Comeback Movie

We're the directors and the leading actors of the movie of our life. In this meditation, we'll go into our subconscious to allow ourselves to witness our own comeback, programming our deepest self for it.

🕐 10–30 minutes or more

1. Find a comfortable position where you can sit or lie down. Close your eyes, and begin focusing on your breath. Allow any stress or tension to leave your body.

2. Let your body relax more and more deeply. If any thoughts arise, let them float away. Bring your focus back to your breath and an even deeper surrender to relaxation.

3. Feel the expansiveness of space all around your body. Feel yourself floating in this endless space. Become one with the infinite space. Take as much time as you need to get here.

4. Allow yourself to witness your own comeback movie. See yourself from this very moment, and watch the montage of events leading you to your next level of life. See all the possibilities coming to you—feel your attitude and energy, and absorb all the excitement of your transformation.

5. Soak it all in. Feel your comeback in every particle of your body. Breathe in gratitude, knowing it's already happening. Sit here for several breaths. Then, open your eyes and live your comeback!

47. Expanding Your Capacity to Receive

Manifesting is more than just attracting—it's also about our ability to receive. Often, we want three dozen roses, but we're only holding out a small water glass to put them in. The more beautiful the things we're ready to call into our life, the bigger the energetic container we need to receive them. This meditation will help you expand your capacity to receive so that your manifestations stick.

🕐 10–30 minutes or more

1. Get into a comfortable, supported, seated position with your back straight and your body relaxed. Close your eyes, and allow your breath to bring you back into your own energy field.

2. Start taking some deep breaths into your heart center, watching the golden ball of light there grow and expand with each breath. Continue until that ball of heart-centered light is covering your entire body. Soak in the love and replenishment of this energy.

3. From this space, ask your inner self, "What is my current capacity to receive?" Notice the level of happiness, abundance, magical opportunities, rich relationships, and so on, that you feel comfortable with in your life right now.

4. Ask your inner self to begin to expand your capacity to receive. Feel what it would be like to hold even more happiness, even more love, even more abundance, even more magic in your being. It may feel a bit uncomfortable, and that's fine. Just breathe into it, and allow your capacity to continue to expand as you sit on the edge of what you're willing to receive. Repeat as many times as you'd like to keep expanding.

5. When you're complete for today's sit, take a minute or two to sit in gratitude for your new capacity to receive. Breathe in, and feel yourself as even more magnetic to your desires after today's practice.

48. Overall Life Feelings Meditation

We discussed the importance of overall life feelings (OLFs) in part I, and the divine vision meditation (Meditation 25, page 45) has helped you clarify what your specific ones are. Now you can put them to work to call in the life you're dreaming of. We want everything we do because of how we think we will feel once it's here. In this meditation, we'll embody those feelings now, embodying our future self and calling in the rest of the details.

1. Relax into a supportive, seated position or lie down, alert, with your eyes closed. (This can be a great meditation to do in bed before you start your day.)

2. Allow your breath to connect you inward with your body. Feel any stress or tension melt away. Take a few minutes to allow your body and breath to synchronize in a state of deep relaxation and openness.

3. Bring your awareness to your third eye (the space just above and between your eyebrows). Feel its energy center activate and open. See it project your future you and feel the OLFs associated with that future you. Your OLFs are just the general emotions you feel about your life on a daily basis—examples are feeling grateful, supported, confident, excited, safe, loved, and inspired.

4. Allow the vision to fade, and focus only on the feelings. Simply breathe, and allow yourself to integrate these feelings deeply into your being for the remainder of your meditation.

5. Take a deep breath in with gratitude, sealing these feelings in your being as you move through the rest of the day.

49. Gratitude Inventory

What we focus on expands. This is the secret of a gratitude practice. It aims our mind in the direction of our abundance, our blessings, and our current joy. The key is keeping it authentic and really feeling how appreciative you are for the things in your life, big and small. This meditation will help you shift your mind-set and align with the frequency of gratitude.

1. Assume a seated position, palms facing up. Close your eyes. Start taking some long, deep breaths, in through your nose and out through your mouth.

2. Begin by feeling gratitude for your breath—your ever-present companion, always supporting you and keeping you alive. Extend your gratitude for the day. What a gift it is each day we have on earth.

3. Next, think of something simple that you're truly grateful for. Maybe it's the soft robe you're wearing this morning, or the smell of the coffee brewing, or the birds chirping outside your window. Pick whatever occurs to you.

4. Continue to extend your gratitude. Which people in your life are you especially grateful for? What opportunities or privileges are you grateful for? Which of your abilities are you truly grateful for? Allow the gratitude to keep flowing, and follow however it naturally shows up on this day.

5. Spend at least 10 minutes soaking up all the blessings and abundance in your life that you're grateful for, big and small.

6. When you're complete, place your hands on your heart and bow your head in gratitude to close your practice.

50. Activating the Frequency of Your Future

Every possibility for your life has a frequency in the quantum field of the universe. Think of it as a giant cell phone network: To reach your phone, someone has to dial a specific number that sends out a signal to connect them to you. The number for you won't reach your friend, your mom, your dad, etc. Each of us has a frequency that correlates to our current life, circumstances, vibration, and so on. This meditation will help you shift your frequency so you can align with the trajectory of your higher vision for your life.

🕐 10–30 minutes or more

1. Get into a relaxed position, sitting or lying down (as long as you won't fall asleep!). Close your eyes. Begin breathing, and allow your body to relax more and more on each exhale.

2. Bring your awareness to your heart center. Continue breathing and letting any external stimuli or distractions fall away as you become one with your heart center in space.

3. Feel the expansiveness of space all around you. Feel yourself melting into the infinite space. Become one with the quantum field of the universe—wide open, warm, loving, boundless, full of potential and possibility. Take as long as you need to arrive here.

4. Now select the new frequency in the field you wish to align with. What is the energy of your future? What is the energy of your dreams fulfilled? It's okay if it's more abstract, like an energy state or feeling. Let it arise naturally when you set the intention to align perfectly with the frequency of your future.

5. Claim this frequency. Let it inhabit your essence in space. Breathe into it. Feel your energy adjusting to it and integrating it. Take several minutes to just be.

6. When you're feeling fully integrated, bring your awareness back into your body. Breathe in and breathe out several times here as you allow your physical body to calibrate to this new frequency. Then, open your eyes and get back to the day.

Meditations to Manifest Radiant Health

This section's meditations are here to help you assist your body in self-healing. They can be used in collaboration with whatever medicine, treatments, or guidance you're receiving from your doctor. They're also great for amping up your vitality and enhancing your body's radiance on a daily basis, even when you're not sick. Whether you're looking to power up your immune system, release excess weight, heal a rash, or simply sleep better, all these meditations infuse your body with a state of love and wholeness that will help you thrive!

51. Your Miraculous Body

The first step to healing our body or increasing our level of vitality is loving and honoring our body. I wrote about this journey in my first book, *Eat with Intention*, and it can be a challenge for many of us to love our body. I have found that honoring how miraculous our body is gets us there authentically.

🕐 10–30 minutes or more

1. Get into a comfortable position, seated or lying down, and close your eyes. Start taking deep breaths in through your nose and out through your mouth.

2. Bring your awareness to your breath. Start breathing in and out with gratitude for your breath. Reflect on how amazing it is that your breath has been supporting your life all these years. Since your first breath outside of your mother's womb until your very last breath at the end of your life, it works tirelessly for you.

3. Next, bring your awareness to your heartbeat. One of the very first signs of your life, your heart has been beating since before you were even born. Your heart pumps blood throughout your entire being, all day and all night. Feel the gratitude you have for your beautiful heart.

4. When you're ready, bring your awareness to the bones that make up your skeleton and the muscles that surround them. They are the framework of your being. They help you walk, dance, give someone a hug, carry groceries, and so much more. Breathe so much gratitude into your muscles and bones.

5. Bring your awareness to your brain and your spinal cord. Give thanks to your nervous system for all it does for your life, day in and day out. Feel gratitude for your sight, your hearing, your sense of touch, your memories, your capacity for critical thinking, and so much more. How blessed you are to have such a miraculous body.

6. Bring your awareness to the entirety of your earth suit. Breathe in awe of all the millions of miracles that go on every day with your cells, organs, and bodily system to allow you to live. Ponder all the messages that are sent within your body each moment so that everything runs smoothly to sustain life. It's incredible. Spend a few minutes in deep gratitude for the miracle of your life.

7. When you're ready to close, place one hand on your navel center and one on your heart, and say a big thank-you.

52. Healing Light Activation

In this meditation, we'll call in divine light to clean and clear any toxins from our body, heal anything that our body needs extra assistance with, and regenerate healthy cells. Scientists believe that light therapy taps into the stored energy and potential within our cells, stimulating the body's innate healing chemistry and allowing for the regeneration of various tissues.

1. Find a comfortable position to sit or lie down. Close your eyes, and completely relax your body. Start taking deep breaths, and let them ease any tension or stress in your body.

2. Notice what areas of your body need a little extra love or are holding on to tension today. Using your breath, breathe into those areas one at a time, allowing your breath to massage the area and ease any tension or pain. Continue with this "massage breath" until you have given some attention to each area that called for it.

3. Now imagine a waterfall of light about two feet above the crown of your head—healing, divine light pouring down all over your body, penetrating through each cell of your being. Picture light going in and cleaning and clearing any cells that are not serving you, any entities in your body that may have been causing harm, and transmuting them all.

4. See the healing light going into every particle of your being and restoring it to perfect health. If a certain area is calling for a little extra love today, see that it receives all this light and comes back online with full health and vitality. See all your cells twinkling with homeostasis and rejuvenation.

5. Feel how this healing has shifted the energy in your body. Feel your divine wholeness. Feel the gratitude you have for your body being able to heal itself, and the ability you have to assist that process.

6. When you're complete, take a deep breath in, hold it, and lock in all these cellular upgrades. Exhale, open your eyes, and take your beautiful body into the day!

53. 528 Hz DNA Repair

The vibration called 528 Hz, a solfeggio frequency, has been used in many civilizations to manifest miracles, bring blessings, and assist the body in self-healing. Solfeggio frequencies, dating back to ancient history, refer to specific tones of sound that help with and promote various aspects of body and mind health. It is said to be the frequency of love, and it has actually been studied to show significant positive effects on our brain. We will use it in this meditation to release stress and assist your body in getting into a mode where it can heal.

🕐 20–30 minutes or more

1. Find a 528 Hz solfeggio frequency track that you enjoy. You can search the many free options available on YouTube or purchase one through iTunes or wherever you get your music.

2. Put on your earphones and press PLAY as you get into a nice, comfortable position lying down. Close your eyes and start taking some deep breaths as you allow yourself to relax and surrender to the music.

3. Continue to keep releasing any tension in your body as you listen. Rest your awareness on your breath. Feel the frequency moving throughout your being, harmonizing each cell, healing any discord, and disseminating love everywhere it reaches. Stay with this for at least 10 minutes. Continue to feel your body and energy field shift as the frequency goes deeper and deeper. If your body falls asleep, it's perfectly fine; trust that it was needed for the healing process.

4. When you're complete, take a few deep breaths into your body and notice how it feels right now. Place your hands with gratitude on your heart, and thank your body for its work.

54. Body Coherence

The body thrives on coherence. Its incredible web of interconnection—from organ system to organ system, cell to cell, and beyond—is what keeps us a well-oiled, running machine. When we're sick, struggling with a medical condition, having a hard time with our digestion, or simply feeling off, it's usually a sign that the body's signaling system is a little jumbled. This meditation is a great way to give your body some love and create the space for it to get back into coherence.

🕐 **10–30 minutes or more**

1. Lie down flat on your back in a relaxing position on the floor, bed, or couch. Close your eyes, and place your hands on your heart and your navel.

2. We'll use what I call an "ocean" breath for this meditation: breathing both in and out through the mouth in a continuous wave. Think of it like the waves crashing on the shore. On the inhale, imagine your breath going in, like the tide dragging the wave back into the ocean. On the exhale, your breath is like the waves crashing onto the beach. They go in and out with a continuous rhythm. Aim to mimic this flow with your mouth breathing.

3. As you breathe, set your intention to connect all the networks in your body into a coherent rhythm with your breath. As you continue, notice any tingling or energy moving in any stuck areas of your body. Let it wake up those areas and get them back online.

4. Continue the breath. See the wave of energy from each breath moving through your entire being, from the top of your head to the bottoms of your toes. See the wave of energy connecting all the cells in your being, rejuvenating them and aligning them with their unique purposes as part of the greater whole.

5. Feel your whole body as one giant system of particles working together in harmony as you take your final few ocean breaths.

6. Release the breath and return to a normal, relaxed, breathing pattern. Feel the shift in energy in your body. Stay here for another few minutes. Allow whatever arises to do so, and whatever needs to integrate to complete before you gently rise.

55. Energy Center Rebalancing

Each energy center, or chakra, connects to a different organ and bodily system. When we experience physical symptoms in our body, we can often correlate it to a blockage or imbalance in one of the energy centers. In this meditation, we'll take our original introduction to energy centers in Meditation 6 (page 24) even deeper, to get your body and your energy back in alignment for perfect health.

🕐 10–30 minutes or more

1. Find a comfortable position, sitting or lying down, and close your eyes. Allow your breath to bring your body to a space of relaxation and surrender before moving to the next step.

2. Bring your attention to your first energy center at the base of your spine, where your sit bone hits your chair. See a beautiful, glowing ball of ruby-red light here. Watch the light grow bigger with each breath as it sends healing energy to all the parts of the body that it is connected with, getting them into alignment.

3. Once your first energy center is bright and vibrant, it's time to move on to the second energy center, about six inches below your navel. Envision a gorgeous ball of deep orange light at this center. Allow your breath to make it expand and glow even brighter as it rebalances and rejuvenates all the areas of the body it presides over.

4. Next, move up to your third energy center, right at your navel center. See a radiant, yellow ball of light. Watch it grow brighter and bigger with each breath you send to it. Allow its light to reach all the organs and glands in this central part of the body.

5. Now move up even higher to our fourth energy center, located at our heart center. Notice its revitalizing emerald-green light growing larger and invigorating the cells in your heart, lungs, and all the other organs, glands, or cells within its reach.

6. Move on to the fifth energy center, located in the center of the throat and glowing with bright, sapphire-blue light. Breathe into this center and watch it expand and shine even brighter. Feel that bright-blue light healing, replenishing, and realigning the entire throat region.

7. Continue upward to your sixth energy center, located at your third eye, or the space about an inch above the area between your eyebrows. Take in the lovely deep indigo–purple ball of light. Once again, send your breath to your entire head to help it thrive and see that light radiate even brighter.

8. Finally, bring your awareness to your seventh energy center, the crown of your head. Take in the glowing ball of light purple–violet light. Allow your breath to assist it in growing even bigger and brighter, strengthening the connection between your physical body and the universe, source, or divine creation energy.

9. Now see all seven of your radiant energy centers glowing with their rainbow of colors. Feel the light of the energy centers touching every cell in your being. Soak this in. Take a deep breath in and hold it, locking in this alignment. Gently bring yourself back into your physical body and into the rest of your day. If you feel the desire to rest afterward, honor your body with a little nap, or simply lie for a bit longer as your body continues its realignment process.

56. Activating Your Most Radiant Body

Our most radiant body already exists as a potential in our energy field. Our body truly desires to be its most radiant and healthy self, so in this meditation we're simply connecting to that version of ourselves and bringing it down into our physical being. The more we reach out and integrate our most radiant body, the more our subconscious mind will direct our actions to help us become it.

🕐 **10–30 minutes or more**

1. Assume a relaxed, seated position with your spine elongated and the rest of your body loose and surrendered. Begin breathing in through your nose and out through your mouth.

2. Bring your awareness to your heart center, and allow your breath to grow and expand your presence there. Let any outside noise or external thoughts simply pass by and fade into the distance.

3. Let your awareness drift deeper inside your heart center until you feel simply like an awareness in infinite space. Feel the boundless space all around you. Take as long as you need to arrive at this feeling.

4. Once you're floating in space, call in the frequency of your most radiant body. What does it feel like? What does it look like? What care and nourishment does it require? Exercise? Food? Sleep? Stress-relieving activities? Notice what naturally arises for you.

5. If you're ready to embody it, consciously decide that you're willing to take on this frequency, with all its facets. Feel the energy of your most radiant body merging with your current energy in the field. Breathe and allow all the upgrades to integrate for several minutes.

6. When complete, feel the feelings of your most radiant body in your entire being for a few minutes. Know that it is activated, and listen to the instructions it has for you to co-create it in your physical reality.

57. Releasing Excess Weight

We all have different shapes, sizes, and comfortable "happy" weights. Don't let a scale, magazine, or outer authority tell you what is right for you. Listen instead to where your body feels the best. We use this meditation for releasing excess weight when we're feeling uncomfortable in our bodies, whether it's from bloating, gaining weight, or inflammation. Our bodies expand to comfort us, keep us safe, and numb out emotional pain. We can release this excess baggage by reminding our bodies that we're safe and can be our most radiant self again.

🕐 **10–30 minutes or more**

1. Begin in a seated or lying-down position (as long as you won't fall asleep). Close your eyes. Place one hand on your navel and another on your heart, and begin breathing deeply.

2. Let your body relax and release any stress or tension it may be holding. Allow your breath to enter any of the spots that need a little extra help to unwind. Get into a deeply surrendered space.

3. Imagine love and light pouring out of the palms of your hands and into your body. Silently say to your body, "Thank you for keeping me safe. Thank you for looking out for me. Thank you for helping me through everything. We are safe. We no longer need this excess weight, inflammation, or bloating to protect us. We are safe now. You are safe to be your most radiant, healthy self. I'm ready and willing to assist you in feeling better than ever." Feel free to riff, and tell your body whatever is in your heart with love and gratitude.

4. When complete, spend a couple of minutes breathing in and out while silently repeating in your mind, "You are safe. It's time to release this excess weight."

5. Feel the energy from your hands going into all the parts of your body and breaking down or releasing anything that is no longer serving it.

6. Finish with a few breaths of love and gratitude for your amazing body, and then honor its needs as you move through the rest of your day.

58. Talk to Your Earth Suit

Your mind can lie, but your body always tells the truth. Our physical body can be a great ally in our health journey if we simply slow down and get quiet enough to listen to it. Our body wants to be in health and harmony. It's programmed to help steer us in the right direction if we open up the communication lines and start listening. This meditation will help you do just that.

🕐 10–30 minutes or more

1. Get into a comfortable, seated position, palms down on your knees, eyes closed, with your awareness on your breath.

2. Set the intention to connect with your earth suit, or the physical body your soul is inhabiting. Place your hands anywhere on your body you feel called to (I usually like the heart and the navel centers). Allow your breath to open up and facilitate this connection to your physical body.

3. Begin by silently apologizing to your body. Make amends for any ways you may have mistreated it, spoken badly about it, or held any resentments against it. Just as with any good relationship, you want to clear the slate before getting into a productive conversation.

4. Next, ask your body what it has been trying to tell you that you haven't been hearing. Allow time for it to answer you. (The more you practice this meditation, the clearer the communication will become.)

5. Ask your body, "What would you like me to do to take better care of you? Is there anything I'm doing that's not working for you? What do you need more or less of?" The mic is yours! Feel free to ask whatever comes to mind, and give your body space to answer you. You may hear an answer or feel a knowing, or you may even get an image. Be open and trust whatever comes up.

6. When you feel complete, thank your body for communicating with you, and assure it that you will take action on the information it shared with you today.

59. Clearing Pain and Discomfort

The body created pain and discomfort to alert us to something awry. Unfortunately, many of us tend to want to eliminate the pain before we've had a chance to hear what the body is trying to communicate. In this meditation, you'll dive deeper into whatever pain or discomfort you're feeling so we can clear it by listening to what it has to tell you.

🕐 10–30 minutes or more

1. Find a comfortable position to relax into for 10 to 20 minutes. Adjust your body, and feel free to use pillows or blankets in whatever way makes your pain or discomfort bearable while we work on releasing it. Close your eyes, and start taking some deep breaths, in through your nose and out through your mouth.

2. Bring your awareness to your breath for a few minutes, and allow any busy thoughts or external noise to gently fall away.

3. When you're ready, bring your awareness to wherever there is pain or discomfort. Choose only one spot at a time. Breathe into the sensation in this area, and intend for your breath to dissipate it more and more with each breath.

4. Let your awareness dive deeper into this discomfort and pain to see what's there. What does it look like? Does it have a color? A shape? Trust whatever naturally comes up for you.

5. Now, as you breathe, allow the color and shape of the pain to rise out of your body, hovering a foot or so above your body. Ask it, "What message do you have for me? Is there something you need me to know? I'm listening." Spend a few minutes here, allowing whatever wants to come through to come through. Don't second-guess anything that arises in your mind—just observe.

6. When you've heard all you need to, let your breath continue to raise the shape and color of this pain or discomfort higher and higher, until it returns to its original frequency in the universe.

7. Fill up its former space with lots of white healing light. Feel gratitude for the pain and discomfort that have left your body. Slowly stretch your body until you're ready to open your eyes.

60. Angelic Healing

Archangel Raphael is the angel of healing. He works to heal people's minds, bodies, and spirits so they can enjoy good health and live their life to the fullest. In this meditation, we'll call on him and any guardian angels we have looking over us to help assist in our healing.

🕐 10–30 minutes or more

1. Get into a supported, seated position, or feel free to lie down if that's more comfortable. Close your eyes, and start taking some nice, deep breaths. Allow your body to completely surrender.

2. Spend a few minutes just focusing on the breath and allowing your mind and body to relax more and more with each inhale and exhale.

3. Now call in Archangel Raphael and your guardian angel(s) by saying something like this: "I now welcome in Archangel Raphael, as well as any angels who are watching over me right now, to assist in my healing [you can insert specifically what your condition is, or leave it open for a whole-body upgrade]. Thank you for your help." Don't worry about saying it word for word; make it your own, and invite any angels or loved ones you'd like.

4. Feel Archangel Raphael's healing emerald light and the violet healing light of your other angels going into your body—into all the areas that need healing energy. Feel the light rebalancing your entire physical being on the cellular level. Feel the angels as they work on your earth suit, removing anything that needs to be removed and recalibrating all that needs to be brought back into order. Allow 10 to 20 minutes for this to fully take place.

5. Intuitively, you'll notice the energy dissipate when the angelic healing is complete. Thank the angels for their assistance, and take a few more deep breaths as you integrate this healing into the new energy of body.

6. Stretch your body in whichever way feels good afterward. Drink plenty of water, and listen to whatever your body may ask for to further support its healing.

Meditations to Manifest Loving Relationships

The meditations in this section will help you experience more loving relationships, both in your romantic life and with your friends or family members. All relationships rise to their best attributes when we come into them as whole individuals who fully love and accept ourselves. While we can't control other people, we can have a profound impact on others and attract the best people into our lives when we take care of our side of the street. Fun fact: The first two meditations are what brought me my now husband! ;)

61. Feeling Deep Romantic Love

"You will know it by the way it feels" is a statement I often repeat to my clients who are searching for romantic love while focusing on what they think it must look like. Just as with all our other manifestations, at the core of our desire is the *feeling* we want to experience. Romantic love is just the same. In this meditation, we'll turn on our magnetism for a romantic partner, or for increasing the love in our current situation, by embodying the feeling now.

🕐 20–30 minutes or more

1. Assume a supported, seated position with your spine long and your body relaxed. Close your eyes, and begin focusing on your breath.

2. Imagine that your love, your partner, is in another part of your home. Maybe they're asleep, or making breakfast, or reading the newspaper with some coffee. Imagine what your dream long-term love is up to while you meditate.

3. Feel their presence in your home. Feel the energy of just knowing they're there.

4. Next, increase your awareness to also feel the love that you two share. How does your love feel? Allow the feeling to wrap you up like a warm blanket, completely enveloping your whole being. Stay here and enjoy this feeling for 10 to 20 minutes.

5. Before closing your meditation, ask yourself, "How would I feel going into my day knowing that this love was already mine?" Open your eyes and act accordingly.

62. Calling in Your Partner

Just as with our other desires, calling in a partner requires us to get really honest about what we truly want in our soul, and then believe that we can have that. This meditation will help you get clear and embody the belief that your dream partner is out there, eager to bump into you!

🕐 10–30 minutes or more

1. Find a comfortable, seated position with your spine elongated and the rest of your body relaxed. Close your eyes and bring your awareness to your heart as you start taking deeper breaths.

2. Rest in your heart space. Allow each breath to bring you deeper and deeper into your heart.

3. Once you're settled into your heart, open up to what your heart truly desires in a partner. What qualities really sing to you? What kind of dynamic do you want between you? What does the communication look like? Don't temper your desires; allow them to be fully accepted and heard.

4. Feel how all the desires being met makes your heart feel, your soul feel. Feel the love, the safety, the excitement of these wishes being fulfilled. Feel this feeling now in every particle of your being. Marinate in this feeling for several minutes before you close this meditation.

5. When you're complete, open your eyes. Grab a journal and write down what surfaced as the most important of your desires—what qualities, what dynamic, and what feelings. Embody these feelings in your daily life right now, even before they arrive.

63. Activating Worthiness

One of the biggest obstacles in the way of forging incredible nourishing and fulfilling relationships is our belief that we're not worthy of them. This applies to romantic and familial relationships and friendships. Events in our past may have led us to believe that we're not worthy of great love or genuine connection. In this meditation, we'll leave that old pattern behind and activate our innate worthiness.

🕐 10–30 minutes or more

1. Find a comfortable, seated position. Close your eyes, relax your body, and focus on your breath.

2. Bring your awareness to your heart center. Let each breath help you surrender more deeply into your heart and release any busy thoughts or external distractions.

3. Continue this breath until you feel that you're just a heart-centered awareness in space. Feel the infinite space on all sides of you. Take as long as you need to get here.

4. Now that you're just your true essence, feel the natural worthiness that is you. Allow yourself to remember the truth that you're worthy of all good things (and so is everyone else on the planet) and that our creator made us powerful creators and placed desires in our hearts to call into our lives. You are worthy by simply existing, and no desire in your heart could conjure up anything that you wouldn't be worthy of receiving.

5. Sit with this realization. Embody the frequency of this worthiness as this core essence. The deepest fabric of who you are is worthy, and no incident or naysayer can ever change that. Continue to breathe and integrate this knowing.

6. Come back into your body. Breathe the frequency of worthiness into every particle of your being. Lock into your physical form the knowing of your essence that you just experienced.

7. When you feel complete, take a few deep breaths in, and notice the shift in your energy. Smile, open your eyes—and go act like the worthy person you've always been!

64. Turning On Your Light

Everyone gives off an energy. When we walk into a room, we can have a green light on that says, "Come say hi to me," or a red light on that says, "Not really in the mood to talk today." When it comes to attracting a romantic partner or even a new friend, it's important to turn on our light and welcome that energy in. This meditation will help you turn on your light and amp up your magnetism for the relationship(s) you're calling in.

🕐 10–30 minutes or more

1. Sit in a comfortable, supported position with your eyes closed and your palms facing up. Begin taking deep breaths in through your nose and out through your mouth.

2. Bring your awareness to the energy field emanating from your heart center and extending all around your being. Continue breathing as you connect with this magnetic field.

3. Set the intention for what you'd like to turn on your light for: a romantic partner, an aligned friendship, or even a great business colleague, for example.

4. Open up your heart to what it would feel like to simply be out and about and to have this person approach you to start up a conversation. Breathe past any discomfort and into the excitement and happiness that would arise from the connection.

5. Feel a bright light turn on in your heart, and watch it emanate outward until your entire field is lit up with this welcoming, warm, attractive energy. Take a few minutes to breathe here as you lock in this light.

6. When you're complete, bring your awareness back inside your body and inside the room. Gently stretch, and open your eyes.

65. Releasing Your Old Patterns

Often the biggest block to manifesting loving relationships is the old patterns that keep playing on repeat. We all have old events in the past—whether previous romantic situations or even as far back as our childhood—that have caused us to believe things about ourselves and the world that sabotage our manifesting deep, long-lasting, loving partnerships. In this meditation, we'll take a look at what past patterns need to be released.

🕐 10–30 minutes or more

1. Sit in a comfortable position with your spine straight, your shoulders relaxed, and your eyes closed. Begin by taking deep breaths, in through your nose and out through your mouth.

2. Allow any stress or worries of the day to wash away with every exhale. Let your breath ease your body into a feeling of deep surrender and relaxation. Take as long as you need to get there.

3. Bring your awareness to your heart center. Feel your breath awakening it and stimulating the emotions of love and being loved.

4. Ask your heart, "What old patterns do I have blocking me from love and receiving love through romantic relationships?" Sit in this question, and allow whatever arises to arise. Don't judge what comes up, just observe it. Feel free to inquire deeper: "Where does that pattern or belief come from?" Get to the bottom of what's coming up.

5. Finally, ask your heart to show you the truth of the matter. What is really *real*, and what is an illusion or a misunderstanding? Let your logical mind get out of the way and allow the answer to come from your heart.

6. Repeat as many times as you like for each pattern or block that comes up. If it feels too intense, do only one per sitting, and come back to release more another time.

7. Feel your heart and your mind releasing the old pattern and sitting in this new truth. Allow the feeling and the knowing of this new truth to permeate your being.

66. Forgiveness Sit-Down

Forgiveness is a secret weapon against everything that's blocking us from what we desire. Whether it's a romantic relationship, a career move, a health shift, or a lifestyle upgrade, if we're stuck in fear, limitation, or doubt, it's because there's someone we need to forgive. This meditation will help you lovingly forgive that person in your life—yourself or even the source, the universe, or your higher power.

When we hold back our forgiveness, we only hurt ourselves by keeping ourselves stuck in a blocked energy pattern. Be willing to forgive, and let your manifestations flow!

🕐 10–30 minutes or more

1. Get into a seated position with your spine elongated and your shoulders down. Close your eyes, and begin breathing in through your nose and out through your mouth.

2. Allow your breath to help you release any tension or stress from your body and mind. Once you feel relaxed, bring your attention down to your heart center, activating it with each breath.

3. In your mind's eye, imagine in front of you the person you need to forgive. (If you need to forgive yourself, this would be another you, and if you need to forgive the universe or source, perhaps the image is a ball of light or something symbolic that resonates with you.) See them sitting a few feet across from you, and make direct eye contact with them.

4. Truly see them from your heart's perspective. See the truth of who they are. The love, the light, the pure essence of creative energy. See their desire to be happy, to be loved, to do the best they can.

5. Set an intention to be willing to forgive them so you can come back into your peace and your power.

6. Now, as you inhale, see them sending loving energy from their heart into yours. As you exhale, imagine that you're sending love from your own heart into theirs. Continue this breathing cycle of giving and receiving love with them for a few minutes or until you genuinely start feeling the love between you.

7. Close by looking them in the eyes once more, smiling and bowing your head to each other. Bring your awareness back into your body, using your breath, and gently open your eyes when you're ready.

67. Love and Acceptance for Your Parental Figures

Who doesn't have a complicated relationship with their parents? People say that they know how to push all your buttons because they're the ones who installed them, and isn't that the truth? Well, healing our relationship with our parents can also have a profound effect on attracting the love and friendships that will be for our highest good. In this meditation, we'll work on loving and accepting your parental figures just as they are.

Tip: This meditation does not require or encourage you to see or contact a parental figure who may be emotionally, psychologically, or physically abusive. You can keep whatever healthy boundaries you need in place while loving and accepting someone on the energetic level.

🕐 **10–30 minutes or more**

1. If you have an old photo of your parental figures when they were young, a nice way to begin this meditation is to simply sit with it and see them. (If you don't, no worries at all—it's not necessary.)

2. Sit in a comfortable, seated position, close your eyes, and begin focusing on your breath. Relax your body and bring your focus internally.

3. Envision a beautiful place in nature, somewhere that feels rejuvenating and healing for you. Take several breaths, enjoying the energy of your special place.

4. Now welcome your parental figures to join you in this beautiful sanctuary. Set your intention to take them in and view them from a higher perspective.

5. Spend several minutes just breathing and truly allowing yourself to see them. See them as other humans, both equally imperfect and divine. See their wounds, their struggles, and their sorrows. Feel their desire to be loved, their efforts to love, and their own yearning to be happy. Sit and allow yourself to see them fully and deeply.

6. When you begin to feel love and acceptance for them just as they are, step toward each one, give them a hug, and whisper, "I love and accept you just the way you are." Feel this love and acceptance coming back from them to you. Sit with this moment.

7. When you're ready, bring your awareness back into your heart center and feel the energy that has shifted in your being.

68. Calling in Your Community

One of the most common desires among my Divinely Design Your Life members is to manifest an amazing group of friends. The older we get, the more intimidating it can feel to make new friends. This meditation will help you turn on your magnetism to align with people who will nourish your soul and enrich your life.

🕐 10–30 minutes or more

1. Get comfortable in a seated position with your back straight and your shoulders relaxed. Close your eyes, and slow your breath to calm and center your body.

2. Bring your awareness to your heart center. Allow your breath to expand and open up your heart's energy field. As you're doing this, allow the desires to arise for what you would like to feel around the people in your friend group or community. What characteristics, energy, or vibes do you want to call in with these soul-aligned friends? What conversations will be sparked? What activities would you enjoy doing together?

3. As your heart's energy field expands, feel the feelings of your desires being fulfilled. Program the intention to magnetize the people who are in the greatest alignment with your journey and your growth into your life right now. Sit with this intention and the feeling of this wish being granted for several minutes.

4. Ask your heart for any wisdom or guidance around finding your community. Is there any action you should take? Any shifts you need to make to call them in? Listen to whatever arises.

5. Bring your hands to your heart and feel the gratitude for the soul-nourishing community coming into your life. Open your eyes, and embrace opportunities throughout the day for connection.

69. To Give Is to Receive

The metaphysical text *A Course in Miracles* says that anything we feel is lacking in a relationship is something that we're not bringing to it. This can be a hard pill to swallow at first, but when we open ourselves up to seeing what it is we need to give, we make way for relationship miracles.

🕐 10–30 minutes or more

1. Sit in a comfortable position with your eyes closed and your body relaxed. Begin breathing in your heart center.

2. As your awareness dives deeper into your heart center with each breath, see yourself inside your heart space at the temple of your heart. Envision this temple in whatever way naturally occurs to you. It is the sacred space within your heart.

3. Bring into this temple with you the person you desire a relationship shift with. It can be a romantic partner, a friend, a parent, a coworker—anyone with whom you need a miraculous relationship shift.

4. Ask yourself what you feel you need from them. What are you wishing they would change, or how do you wish they would behave?

5. Now ask yourself, "How could I give this person what I'm yearning to receive in this relationship?" Stay open, and be willing to hear what comes forth. Keep breathing into your heart center as you allow for whatever needs to arise.

6. When you realize what you need to do, tell the other person what you have discovered. If possible, show them a gesture of what you're now willing to give.

7. Feel the feelings of receiving the gift you're now willing to give.

8. Bring your awareness back into your heart, back into your body, and slowly open your eyes. Take action on your heart-centered guidance in this relationship.

70. Feeling the Love

In this meditation, we'll use a mudra (hand gesture) for activating our heart chakra to feel the love that we all innately exude and the love we yearn to receive from others. When we're able to create the feeling of being loved from within, we attract healthier relationships in which two whole beings come together to enrich each other's life.

🕐 10–30 minutes or more

1. Sit cross-legged on the floor. Touch your thumb to your index fingers, place your right hand at your heart center, and rest your left hand on your knee.

2. Begin breathing and bringing your awareness to your heart center. Feel your heart's energy awaken and expand.

3. Notice feelings of deep love, acceptance, and compassion flowing throughout your being. With each breath, feel this love, acceptance, and compassion grow more and more. Continue for 10 to 20 minutes, until you feel that your entire being is love, wrapped in love, and radiating love.

4. When you're complete, take in three deep breaths with gratitude. Hold each breath for a few seconds before exhaling to lock this feeling within your being.

Meditations to Manifest Financial Abundance

Manifesting financial abundance starts from the inside out. We often feel as if we hustle our way to prosperity, but the truth is, if you don't believe you're worthy of money, it will always flow out of your hands even if you do receive it. In the meditations in this section, you'll release any anxiety, limiting beliefs, and shame you may have in relation to money, and step into the frequency of abundance and wealth. You'll need to take action to call in money, of course, but these meditations will ensure that you're taking the right, aligned actions.

71. Your Inner CEO

To call in money, we need to both energetically and literally be responsible hands to hold the amount of money we wish to have. So often, we desire large sums of money when we're not even being a good steward of the small sums we currently have. Each new level of financial prosperity involves us stepping up to a new level of responsibility with regard to our wealth. In this meditation, we'll tap into our "inner CEO" to illuminate any blind spots in how we deal with our finances.

🕐 10–30 minutes or more

1. Get into a comfortable, seated position with your eyes closed and your shoulders relaxed. Begin taking long, deep breaths, in through your nose and out through your mouth.

2. Bring your awareness to the core of your being, around your navel center, and imagine a ball of golden light there. As you breathe in and out, see the ball of light glow and expand as it activates the core of your being.

3. Allow the external world and any thoughts about the day to melt away as you become one with that ball of light. Sense the space all around you, and feel the warmth of the light in your being.

4. Set the intention to call on your inner CEO, or the part of you that represents your most responsible and evolved self when it comes to money and business. Ask this part of you to show you what they might do differently in your life. See them handling your finances, managing large sums of money, and growing your net worth.

5. Relax and allow yourself to receive whatever wisdom, visions, or thoughts are coming through around how you could step into your next-level, financially responsible self.

6. Feel free to ask this inner CEO of yours for any guidance you may need regarding specific circumstances. When you feel complete, bring your awareness back to your breath and your body.

7. Take a few moments to ground back into your body. Gently begin to stretch your arms and open your eyes. Grab your notebook and write down what came through from today's meditation.

72. Calling in a Money Miracle

We all have a relationship with money; whether it's good or bad, it's there, and it affects us every day. In this meditation, we'll bring this mostly subconscious relationship into our awareness so we can look at what our dynamic has been with money and make a shift in our perception—in other words, experience a miracle around our experience of money.

1. Begin this meditation by holding a dollar bill in your hands and looking straight down at it. Or you can use whatever bill denomination you have. Take a few minutes to simply breathe while observing this dollar bill in your hand, and notice what comes up for you. How do you feel? What thoughts come up as you look at this money?

2. When you're ready, close your eyes while holding the money, and ask yourself, "What do I really think about money? What kind of relationship do we have?" Don't overanalyze or hold anything back—just recognize what your natural instincts have to say about money and how you feel about it.

3. Some complicated emotions may come up for you when you're thinking about your relationship with money. Feel them with compassion. Allow yourself to fully witness how you honestly feel and what you believe about the dynamic between money and you.

4. Once you feel complete in that understanding, it's time to ask for a miracle. Say to your soul, source, the universe, or the divine, "I am ready to see things differently. I need a money miracle. I want to have a loving, nourishing relationship with money." Breathe into this request, and give yourself space to receive whatever wants to come through.

5. Gently open your eyes and see that dollar bill once again. This time, feel your heart fill up with love and gratitude for money. Think of all the beautiful ways that it supports you, feeds you, provides you with clothes, shelter, and so on. Breathe for a few minutes, just allowing yourself to feel the love of money.

6. When you're complete, bring the dollar bill up to your heart center, take a deep breath, and commit to a new relationship with money moving forward.

73. Breaking the Chain of Lack

Many of us grew up in families with a long lineage of poverty, struggle, and frustrations with money. Even though our parents and grandparents did everything they could to make sure that wasn't our personal experience, we still inherited a lot of those beliefs about money. In this meditation, we'll tap into what money beliefs we inherited from our family that are no longer relevant for us.

🕐 10–30 minutes or more

1. Find a relaxed position to sit in. Close your eyes, and allow your breath to bring your focus inward.

2. Let thoughts from the day float away as you keep your awareness on your breath and continue to relax your body into a deep surrender. Continue until you feel as if you're a floating breath in a sea of space with everything else melted away.

3. Call on the energy of your ancestors—the lineages of your mother, father, their parents, and so on. Through your mind's eye, see their relationship with work or money. Feel how they felt about money. Observe it all with compassion.

4. When you're ready, tell them you're ready to break the chain. Tell them that you appreciate all they've done to get you to this moment, and now you're going to flip the family script to one of abundance. Set the intention to send any lack of energy or programming in your being back to them, where it originated. Feel it being released.

5. When you're complete, feel the blessings of your ancestors to blaze the new path of abundance forward. Feel their excitement for you, and feel your own gratitude for doing the work and embracing this new energy regarding work and money. Stay here for a few minutes to let it marinate.

74. Releasing Anxiety, Stress, and Negative Feelings about Money

The most common way we repel money is through the negative feelings we associate with it. If you had a friend who made you feel horrible every time they came around, you probably wouldn't want to spend a lot of time with them, right? The same goes for money. We need to release our negative associations with money so we can call in the abundance that we crave and that belongs to us.

🕐 **10–30 minutes or more**

1. Get into a seated position. If you're in a chair, place both feet on the floor. Close your eyes, and place your hands, palms down, on your knees. Take some long, deep breaths.

2. Allow whatever negative feelings you're currently experiencing with regard to money to arise. Notice where they are in your body, what memories come up around them, and what thoughts they trigger. Begin alternating hands and tapping on your knees while you do this (right palm tapping on right knee, then left palm tapping on left knee, alternating taps on each knee throughout the meditation).

3. Notice how your thoughts, feelings, and memories may morph or shift as you continue to breathe and tap on your knees for several minutes. When you feel peaceful regarding money, stop the tapping for a couple of minutes and just breathe.

4. Now ask yourself honestly, "Do I have any fear, shame, or anxiety about *being wealthy*?" (For example, what if everyone asks me for money, or what if I have to pay a ton in taxes, or what if I don't invest it wisely . . . ?) Allow anything to arise, and feel it all.

5. Begin tapping alternate knees again. Let the thoughts, feelings, and images around your wealthy worries flow as you continue to take deep breaths and move through them.

6. When you find yourself in a more peaceful place and you feel complete, stop tapping and just breathe into your heart. On every exhale, release any of that old energy that you transmuted. Do this for a few minutes, and then gently open your eyes and wake up your body.

75. Connecting to the Frequency of Abundance

When we think of abundance, we often associate it with material goods or money. However, abundance is just a frequency in the quantum field—it's something that all of us have access to. What does abundance feel like to you? Is it feeling free to do whatever you want? Is it feeling supported to truly nourish and take care of yourself? In this meditation, we'll connect with the frequency of abundance and what that vibration feels like for us specifically.

🕐 20–30 minutes or more

1. Get into a comfortable, seated position. Relax your body and close your eyes. Let your breath help you release any tension in your body and clear your mind.

2. Bring your awareness to your heart center, letting everything else melt away from your consciousness so that you're simply a breath in your heart space. Surrender deeper and deeper into this space.

3. Notice the infinite space on either side of you and above and below you. Feel like a floating essence in boundless space. Breathe and rest here for a few minutes, allowing yourself to transcend deeper and deeper into the nothingness.

4. Awaken the energy and frequency of abundance from within you. What does abundance feel like to you? Is it freedom? Is it creativity? Is it nourishment? Observe the essence of your desired abundance. When you find it, feel this feeling in every particle of your being, seeing the images of this playing out in your mind's eye. Stay here for 10 to 15 minutes, crystallizing this frequency into your being.

5. When you're complete, bring your breathing back into your body. Come back into the room, and gently take your time opening your eyes. Keep the energy of abundance with you as you move through your day.

76. Allowing Money to Flow

Money is not meant to stay stagnant—it's energy, and it's meant to flow. When we allow the natural flow of money coming to us and going out toward goods and services that enrich our lives, the flow increases. When we stop the flow because we have shifted into a place of lack and scarcity, we also stop the flow coming in. This meditation will help you release your tight grasp on money and open up the flow to receive more.

🕐 20–30 minutes or more

1. Get into a comfortable, seated position, and place your right palm facing up on your knee in a gesture of receiving. Hold your left hand up (as if holding up a stop sign or raising your hand half-way), with your palm facing outward, in a gesture of giving. Close your eyes.

2. As you begin to inhale, imagine energy coming into your being through the palm of your right hand. As you exhale, see energy coming out and going back into the universe through your left hand. Continue this for several minutes to get into a good rhythm with the flow of energy coming in and going out.

3. Once you've got the flow, add in the feeling that this energy is money, and whatever other abundance you're calling in. Feel yourself fully receiving it with your right hand, experience its energy in your being, and then feel yourself giving that abundance joyfully out of your left hand. Perhaps your left hand is paying the mortgage on a beautiful house, paying off a bill after a whirlwind vacation, or donating to your favorite charity.

4. Continue breathing and experiencing the flow of money in and out for 10 to 15 minutes. Challenge yourself to feel your body relaxed and happy with receiving more and giving more. Push your own limits of what you thought might be comfortable on either end.

5. When you're ready, place both hands over your heart for several ending breaths. Feel the love and gratitude in your heart for the flow of money in your life.

77. Wondrous Wealth + Success Visualization

When we're stuck in our old money story, it can feel almost painful to truly let ourselves fantasize about having incredible wealth. Yet, when we don't allow ourselves to feel the feelings and see what that level of abundance or success looks like for us, how can we expect to align with it energetically? In this meditation, you'll treat yourself to a vision of wondrous wealth, and you'll get to saturate yourself in the images, feelings, and thoughts of your most financially abundant self!

🕐 20–30 minutes or more

1. Get into a relaxed position, either sitting or lying down. Close your eyes, and allow your breath to help you turn your awareness from the external world to your internal world.

2. Allow your awareness to rest deep inside your heart space. Feel your physical body and the external world melting away as you rest in this infinite place inside.

3. When you're there, ask your heart to show you what true wealth and success look like to your soul. Open yourself up to whatever thoughts, images, and words arise to share your heart's truth with you.

4. Observe all the exciting things you might do: what upgrades would be made in your life; how you would feel about work, money, and yourself—soak it all in. Stay in this alternate reality of your wealth and success for the next 10 to 15 minutes, enjoying every moment.

5. When you're complete, take several breaths in and out. Lock in this vision and feeling in every particle of your body. When you open your eyes, jot down any earthly actions that may have come up for you to take.

78. Manifesting a Specific Amount of Money

For this meditation, we'll do a simple version of an exercise called emotional freedom technique (EFT). Think of EFT as psychological acupressure. We'll use one of the many tapping points as a tool to shift our energy to call in a specific amount of money.

🕐 10–30 minutes or more

1. Decide what amount of money you'd like to manifest and how you want it to show up. For example, I want $50,000 in my savings account, or I want to receive a check for $5,000.

2. Hold your left hand in a karate chop–like position, fingers pointing upward, about six inches in front of your heart. With the fingertips of your right hand, tap along the side of the left hand, below the pinky finger.

3. Breathe and tap the entire time while you say these statements aloud:

- "Even though I don't yet have X (= amount of money) in/ from Y (= specific place), I still love and accept myself."
- "I know the only reason I haven't received XY is because I must be blocking it."
- "Something in my energy, my field, or my belief system must be pushing it away."
- "But I'm ready to release whatever has been blocking it now because I'm completely ready to receive XY."
- "I'm releasing anything in my DNA and cellular memory that is stopping me from manifesting XY."
- "I am opening up my energy field to receive XY in record time."
- "I am entirely capable of manifesting XY."
- "I am a divine creator of my reality. Money is just another form of energy that I can align with."
- "I am recalibrating my body, mind, and soul to align with receiving XY."
- "I am excited to receive XY and trust that it is on its way. And so it is!"

4. Feel free to add in any messages that ring true to what's coming up for you, and make them your own. The general feeling should be you accepting ownership for your reality and therefore choosing to change it. When you're finished, take a few deep breaths and drink some water before getting back to your day. You moved more energy than you may realize!

79. The Ocean of Infinite Abundance

Abundance is all around us. It's the true nature of our world. You can see abundance in the grass, in the beach, in the sky, or in the ocean—Mother Earth is full of abundance when you adjust your eyes to see it. In this meditation, you'll allow yourself to see it all around you and experience more abundance in your life as it makes its way to you!

🕐 **20–30 minutes or more**

1. Get into a relaxed position, sitting or lying down. Fully surrender your body and close your eyes. Take some slow, deep breaths.

2. With each breath, release more tension from your body. Allow your thoughts to fade away as you sink deeper into your internal self.

3. In your mind's eye, see yourself standing on the beach in front of a beautiful ocean. Take a moment to feel the sand under your feet, the gentle salt-air breeze, and the sound of the waves crashing before you. Stare out into the horizon of the ocean, receiving its transmission of abundance. Stay here for a few minutes.

4. Next, begin walking into the water. It's your favorite temperature and glistens under the sun. As you make your way out beyond the break, lean back and allow yourself to float in its salty, healing goodness. Feel the water supporting you, and see the water extending toward the horizon. Embrace the abundance you're floating in.

5. As you continue floating, expand your awareness of the ocean's abundance to all abundance. Feel all your heart's desires and the infinite possibilities for how they could manifest in your life all around you. Envision yourself floating in a sea of money, opportunity, and blessings. Float here for another 10 minutes, really relaxing into your ocean of abundance.

6. When you feel complete, bring your awareness back into your body. Spend a few minutes feeling the abundance and opportunities in your being before opening your eyes.

80. Walking into Wealth

By now, you know what it feels like to sit in meditation and align with the vibration of financial abundance. The next step is actually integrating that energy into your day-to-day life. In this walking meditation, you'll get up and go out into the world, continuing to do the inner work to lock in your next level of wealth.

🕐 20–30 minutes or more

1. Find a safe walking path for your journey. Begin by standing still with your hands on your heart center. Close your eyes, and take some deep breaths in and out, grounding yourself in the moment.

2. Keep your awareness in your heart space and allow the world to fall away as you rest here for just a few minutes. As you breathe in and out, activate the vision and feeling in your heart of what true wealth and prosperity feel like for you.

3. Let this vision and the feelings evoked by it bubble up inside your heart with joy and excitement. When you're ready, open your eyes slightly and fix your focus on the horizon as you walk forward into your future wealth.

4. While you walk forward, feel free to put on music that moves you emotionally and enhances your feelings of abundance, success, wealth, joy, or love. Embody the energy of your wealthiest self as you move forward. Feel how your posture, your energy, and even the thoughts in your head shift to align with the vibration of abundance. Continue walking for another 10 to 20 minutes, or as long as you'd like.

5. When you're complete, return to standing still. Close your eyes and place your hands on your heart. Take several breaths here, just filling yourself up with gratitude for the wealth that is on its way to you.

Meditations for Manifesting a Purposeful Career and Making an Impact

We're all here for a purpose and create an impact with the way we live our lives. Just as our desires are divinely designed for our highest soul experience of this life, so is our career. The dreams we have concerning the work we do in the world and the difference we can make are not an accident. They are here for us to bring them to life. This section's meditations will help you do just that.

81. Connecting to Your Divine Purpose

All of us come here with one divine purpose: to be loved and to give love. However, the way we show up for our purpose and how that manifests career-wise are different for each one of us. This meditation will help you connect to the unique way your purpose wants to move through you.

🕐 10–30 minutes or more

1. Find a supported, seated position with your eyes closed and your palms facing up. Begin by taking deep breaths in through your nose and out through your mouth.

2. Release any stress or tension in your body with each breath, and allow any thoughts to float by in your mind as you recenter into your internal peace.

3. Bring your awareness to your solar plexus chakra or navel energy center. See a bright ball of golden yellow light here, glowing and expanding with each breath.

4. As you're activating your third energy center, or chakra, which is connected to your sense of personal power and purpose, notice what thoughts naturally arise from within. Do images, words, or thoughts about a certain occupation, activity, or area of study arise?

5. Ask your soul, "What do I truly feel called to do? To share with the world? What gifts have I been given to use?" Honor whatever arises—try to release your rational thoughts and logic so you can be wide open to all answers. Sit here honoring all that is coming up into your mind's eye for 10 to 15 minutes.

6. When you feel complete, bring your breath back into your being and ground yourself back into the room. Open your eyes and grab a journal to write down everything that arose in the meditation. Keep doing this meditation regularly for more and more clarity.

82. Calling in Your Soul-Aligned Career

Perhaps you already know what your soul-aligned career is, or at least what it would feel like when you're doing it (either will work!), but you feel a bit lost on how to get from where you are right now to the career of your dreams. This meditation will help you call in that career and align you with any opportunities or next steps to take.

1. Sit in a comfortable position. Close your eyes, focus on your breath, and allow your body to relax.

2. Bring your awareness to your heart center. Let everything else melt away. Let the outer world, your physical body, and any busy thoughts evaporate as you continue to focus on your heart space and your breath.

3. Bring up the feelings of your soul-aligned career. Feel how it will feel when it's your reality. See any images and hear any thoughts that relate to it. Saturate yourself in this energy for 10 to 15 minutes.

4. When you're complete, place your hands on your heart. Feel gratitude for this new soul-aligned career that is on its way to you. Sit in gratitude for several minutes.

5. Open your eyes and grab your journal. Write down any guidance or aligned actions that arose for you to take during your meditation.

83. Manifesting a Level Up in Your Career

You're reading this book right now because you're committed to growth. You constantly want to push the boundaries for what you can do in this one wild and precious life. Up-leveling is a natural part of our soul's expansion, and this meditation will assist you in manifesting the next step in your career evolution.

1. Find a comfortable, seated position and close your eyes. Turn your awareness inward with long, deep breaths.

2. Bring your focus to your mind's eye, or your sixth energy center—about an inch up from the space between your eyebrows. Allow your inhales and exhales to activate and expand this center. See it as a ball of deep purple light, spinning and glowing.

3. Watch as the beautiful purple light of your sixth energy center grows and expands to encompass your entire being.

4. Ask this most intuitive part of yourself to show you what the next level of your career holds. Relax, and receive and honor whatever arises. Notice what feelings are present in the next evolution—what projects you're working on and any other distinct details.

5. Take several minutes to lock in this next level in your being. Feel it crystallizing in your cells and DNA. Your whole being is ready for the upgrade; open up to receive it.

6. Ask your intuitive guidance for any wisdom or direction. Is there anything that you should be doing yourself? Does the universe want you to surrender or release something?

7. When you're complete, bring your breath back into your body, and open your eyes. Trust that your next level is on its way, and take any intuitive action that you were guided to.

84. Owning Your Impact

We're all here to make an impact on the world. Sometimes that impact comes out in our career, and sometimes it comes out in our side projects or volunteer work. Most often, it arises from how we show up as a person in our interactions throughout our days. This meditation will help you center on the impact that you can make.

1. Get into a comfortable, seated position. Close your eyes and begin breathing in through your nose and out through your mouth.

2. Bring your awareness to your heart center. Feel it expand and grow with every breath. Let the feelings of your heart rise up to your consciousness—the love, the truth, the acceptance, and the interconnectedness of us all. Give yourself a few minutes to bask in these feelings.

3. Let the outside world fall away. Allow your thoughts to dissipate and your entire being to rest in your heart space with its boundless love and deep soul-aligned truth.

4. Set the intention to feel, see, and hear the impact you're here to create. What effect will your energy, your presence, and your actions have on the world? Sit here for several minutes and see what arises.

5. If you need further clarification, ask whatever questions may be arising for you, and honor what comes up in response.

6. Finally, ground yourself into the energy of the you who's making an impact on the world simply by how you show up for your life. This is the largest impact we make, and it's from this energy that all other versions of our impact on the world originate. Spend several minutes saturating yourself in this energy.

7. When you're complete, gently stretch or move your body to wake it up. Open your eyes and write down in your journal anything significant that you want to remember.

85. Birthing a New Project

Whether it's a business, a book, or a new presentation you've been tasked to create at work, this meditation will help you tap into your creative center to birth the project that will make your soul sing. It will also help you get any clarity or direction you might need along the way.

🕐 **10–30 minutes or more**

1. Sit in a comfortable position with your spine elongated and your shoulders back and down. Close your eyes, and begin breathing in through your nose, out through your mouth.

2. Witness your body relaxing more and more with each breath. Let any thoughts coming up in your mind gently pass by like clouds in the sky, bringing you gently back to your breath.

3. Focus your awareness on your sacral chakra, or second energy center, about six inches below your navel. Breathe into this area and see a beautiful, sunset-orange ball of water, growing and glowing with each breath.

4. Allow your consciousness to dive into this magnificent orange ocean of creation energy. Hold the intention of the project you're ready to birth in your consciousness in this space, and simply notice what arises.

5. Ask your creative center to show you whatever you need to know about birthing this project into life, and any direction it may want to share with you. Sit here and allow yourself to fully receive all that wants to come forth for 10 to 15 minutes.

6. When you feel complete, bring your awareness back into your body for a few breaths, grateful for the wisdom you've received. When you're ready, open your eyes, grab your journal, and write down everything that came through.

86. From Nervous to Service

In my heart-centered business program, "Spread Your Light," one of the most common questions I get is this: "How do I overcome my nervousness about speaking engagements?" People have similar questions about handling their nerves when they share a story on social media, start a podcast, ask their boss for more responsibility, give a presentation, and so on. My reply is always, "When you're nervous, it's a sign that you need to start focusing on service." When we focus on how we're here to serve through our actions, we get out of our own way and focus on the job at hand. This meditation will help you do just that!

🕐 10–30 minutes or more

1. You can do this meditation anywhere you have between 5 and 15 minutes. It will allow you to get your head out of the way and put your heart in the driver's seat before a big talk, presentation, or any situation that has you feeling nervous. Begin by closing your eyes, placing your hand on your heart, and taking slow, deep breaths.

2. Think about the event or circumstance at hand. Allow all the feelings you may be experiencing about it to come up. Gently and compassionately breathe through the emotions, and continue to center yourself.

3. Now ask your heart, "Who am I here to help? What impact can I make today?" Spend a few minutes acknowledging what comes up.

4. Then focus even deeper: "How can the work I'm here to do today be truly helpful? How can I make sure that the people who really need to hear this understand me? Is there anything else I need to know about what I'm sharing or need to share?" Breathe and await the answers. Honor whatever arises.

5. Finally, envision yourself successfully making the presentation—or handling the situation—and really seeing how it affects those people it was helpful to. Enjoy this feeling for a few minutes before opening your eyes and getting into heart-centered, service-focused action!

87. The Courage to Follow What Lights You Up

We're rigged so divinely for success, yet so many of us get in our own way by falling prey to the status quo. The things that light us up, that set our heart abuzz, are not random. They are directions on how we're meant to spend this life—the gifts we have and what we're here to share. This meditation will help you find the courage to listen to what is lighting you up.

🕐 **10–30 minutes or more**

1. Find a comfortable, seated position with your eyes closed and your body relaxed. Start breathing in through your nose and out through your mouth as your body relaxes further. Turn your attention inward.

2. Bring your awareness to your heart center. Let your heart center open and expand with each breath. Feel the love and light residing here in your soul space.

3. Ask your heart, "What truly lights me up? What activities do I really lose myself in? What subjects am I endlessly interested in reading about or discussing? Where do I feel like my best self? What brings out my creativity, my joy, and has me losing track of time?" Sit here for 10 to 15 minutes, allowing whatever surfaces to arise. Sit with it. Observe it without judging or overthinking.

4. Take the next few minutes to simply breathe into your heart and sit with what has come through for you. Notice whether any fears or doubts come up for you. Sit back and witness these fears or doubts as the observer, without identifying with them.

5. Feel the fears and allow the love and passion in your heart to slowly dissipate them more and more with each breath. Stay here as you transmute your fears to courage to go after what lights you up.

6. When you're complete, bring your awareness back into your body and back into the room. Open your eyes, grab your journal, and jot down what came through for you in this meditation.

88. Connecting with Those You're Here to Help

Regardless of our career path, we're all here to be love to each other. As Ram Das famously said, "We are all just walking each other home." When we connect to those we're here to help, it can reinvigorate a lackluster career situation or be a powerful force of creation for a new career endeavor we wish to embark on. This meditation will help strengthen the connection between you and the people you serve with your work.

🕐 10–30 minutes or more

1. Get into a comfortable, seated position with your eyes closed and your spine straight. Begin breathing into your heart center.

2. Let any thoughts flow by like waves going back out to sea. Let any external distractions become quieter and quieter with each breath. Allow your consciousness to relax deeply in your heart space.

3. In your mind's eye, bring up an image of the people you're here to help. It could be just one person who's symbolic of the group, or you may see a whole group. Either is perfect. Witness who came forth, and sit with them. Breathe in their energy, their circumstances, their situation, and the desires of their heart.

4. Feel a cord of light connecting your heart to their heart. Sense what their heart is asking for and what you can provide or how you can uplift. Send a transmission from your heart to their heart, letting them know whatever your heart wants to tell them.

5. When you feel complete, open your heart to receive a transmission back from them. What does their heart want to tell you? Sit and receive whatever comes through.

6. Take a final look into the eyes of the people you're here to serve, and thank them for being part of your journey in this lifetime. Bring your awareness back into your body. Slowly open your eyes, and take action on your newfound insights.

89. Incredible Alignment

Alignment is a manifestation expeditor! When I was in my early 20s, a yoga teacher said to us in class, "How might you show up differently if you acted like you were the most influential person in the world?" At first I thought it was preposterous, but it really stuck with me. So I pretended that I was on a reality show 24/7. I acted in alignment with my values, presenting the best version of myself. My life changed dramatically once I got to that level of radical alignment. This meditation will help you do the same and rocket-launch those manifestations in!

1. Find a supported, seated or lying-down position. Relax your body and close your eyes. Allow each breath to help you surrender more and more as your physical body relaxes and melts away.

2. Feel yourself floating in infinite space. Notice the space in front of you, behind you, and to each side of you. Allow yourself to sink into the infinite abyss. Take as long as you need to get here.

3. Set the intention to see what it would look like if you lived in complete alignment with your truth, values, and the message you'd like to send out to others. Spend several minutes here noticing what arises.

4. Once you feel fully in tune with what has come through, ask yourself, "Where are the areas right now where I'm not living in alignment with my highest self?" Sit here and compassionately observe what comes up.

5. When you're ready, once again rest in your heart space. What are you committed to shifting, changing, or incorporating into your lifestyle to live more in alignment with your highest self? Breathe into the shifts that are ready to be made in your world.

6. Take several deep breaths in gratitude for this attunement into greater alignment that is assisting you in bringing the life you've been dreaming of into reality.

90. Turning On Your Magnetism

Ever wonder why some people naturally get noticed for their thoughts, efforts, and good work? It's an essence of magnetism that comes from confidence, self-worth, and trust in their own talents and abilities. This is what opens them up to receive recognition, attention, and customers for their work. In this meditation, we'll turn on your career magnetism.

1. Get into a comfortable, seated position, close your eyes, and begin breathing in and out through your mouth. Let your entire body relax as your breathing cleans and clears out any tension or stress.

2. Clear your mind, and focus only on your breath as it deeply shifts the energy in your body. Notice how your body surrenders as you drift out into spaciousness.

3. Feel your being just floating in spaciousness as the world around you melts away. Imagine the very essence of your being as a giant ball of light with a powerful magnet inside. As your breath makes this ball of light grow brighter and brighter, the magnet inside is growing stronger and stronger.

4. Sense your innate magnetism radiating outward from the ball of light that is your very essence. Feel it attracting aligned opportunities, acknowledgments, recognition, and people who would be served by your work. Let yourself bask in the feeling of being a magnet and drawing everything to you with your career. What would shift? How does it feel? What are you sure of about yourself and your abilities?

5. Spend several minutes aligning with the frequency of this expanded magnetism and the power of it turning up from the very core of your being. Let it crystallize in every particle of your being.

6. When you're complete, begin breathing naturally again through your nose and mouth. Reintegrate into your body, and slowly open your eyes.

Meditations for Manifesting Miracles, Synchronicities, Magical Opportunities

This section is for those of you advancing on your meditation path and ready to incorporate more general up-leveling and magic-making tools into your day-to-day life. All the meditations in this section will greatly assist you with whatever manifestation you're currently working with. They could be your secret sauce for overcoming any hurdles along the way.

91. Asking for the Miracle

As defined by the metaphysical text *A Course in Miracles*, a miracle is a shift in perception from fear to love. When we feel stuck in fear, limitation, or frustration, it's our cue to ask for the miracle to help us see the situation clearly. Being able to see through the eyes of love also aligns us with our manifestation powers again, since we can't create our own reality when we're stuck in a place of fear or lack. This meditation will help midwife your miracle and get your mind back into its manifestation sweet spot.

🕐 10–30 minutes or more

1. Sit in a comfortable position with your eyes closed, and begin breathing into your heart center.

2. Set the intention for the situation for which you need a miracle by saying, "Dear Universe [or God/Source/Divine/etc.]: I need a miracle. I'm not seeing the situation involving XYZ clearly, but I am willing to see it differently."

3. Hold the situation at hand gently in your mind's eye as you allow a wave of love, compassion, abundance, and infinite possibilities to wash over you. Breathe it in, and see how your view of the situation changes as this new energy integrates.

4. Sit here for 10 minutes or so. Continue to breathe into your heart center. Hold the situation, along with the loving, expansive feelings of your higher knowing, and simply see what emerges.

5. When you have received the miracle (the shift in your perception), bring your hands to your heart, and take several breaths in gratitude for returning to your true vision. If you don't receive a shift during your meditation, still put your hands on your heart and feel gratitude for the shift, trusting that it will come to you during the day.

92. Surrendering to Synchronicity

Synchronicity is when meaningful events happen in serendipitous ways in our lives. These events often attune us to the divine or the universe working in mysterious ways with our greatest intentions in mind. When we surrender to synchronicity, we open ourselves to the possibility that things can come into our life in magical and unconventional ways. In this meditation, we'll release the practical ways that we assume our manifestation has to come to us, and make way for otherworldly occurrences.

🕐 10–30 minutes or more

1. Find a supported, seated or lying-down position. Close your eyes, and begin taking deep breaths in through your nose and out through your mouth. Bring your focus to your inner world.

2. Allow any stress or tension to leave your body, and clear your mind of any busy thoughts with every inhale and exhale. Sink deeper into surrender.

3. Feel your physical body melt away, and experience yourself as a floating essence in nothingness, in endless space. Take your time to relax into this feeling.

4. See your desire as a small, golden ball of light, floating in this endless space. Feel its energy, the energy of this desire being manifest in your life.

5. Now witness the tiny lightning-like constellations leading to it from every direction. Witness a gold string tying other small golden-ball events together, leading into your desire. See the beautiful geometric patterns of possibility for all the ways the divine could orchestrate your desire manifesting. Sit here for 10 to 15 minutes.

6. Ground yourself into an enormous sense of trust that it is all unfolding as it should, and an openness to all the magical ways it could come into your life. Stay here for several closing breaths, and then open your eyes.

93. Toroidal Energy Field Activation

Toroidal energy fields are electromagnetic fields given off from our heart space. They exist around everything from humans to trees because it is from this field that everything is created. Our field contains two toruses, one spiraling upward and one spiraling downward, constantly refreshing themselves. When we activate this center of creation, we can supercharge our manifestations.

🕐 10–30 minutes or more

1. Get into a comfortable, seated position with your eyes closed.

2. Bring your awareness to your breath. Let any thoughts or outside distractions float away as you keep returning to the breath.

3. Envision your own toroidal field: Think of it like the shape of an apple or a doughnut with energy pulling upward from your root center to your crown and then cascading over and around again. Feel your field collecting from the infinite and bringing your desires into your personal field up through your root to your crown, overflowing and back again.

4. Continue with this practice, allowing yourself to feel the flow of your desires and abundance moving into your field. Feel the power of the regenerative cycle of your toroidal field. Do this for several more minutes.

5. When you're complete, refocus on your breath as you come back into your physical body. Integrate this new level of expansion and abundance into your being for a few minutes before you open your eyes.

94. Meeting Your Guardian Angel

Every one of us has a guardian angel. They're part of our spirit support squad, but they can't intervene with our lives unless we ask for help. If you're a believer, this meditation will help you get to know your guardian angel and invite them to assist you in your manifestations.

🕐 10–30 minutes or more

1. Get into a comfortable, seated position, close your eyes, and begin focusing on your breath. Allow your body to relax and your thoughts to quiet as you surrender more and more to your breath.

2. Set the intention to call in your guardian angel. Bring your awareness to your heart center and see a glowing ball of golden light there, growing larger with each inhale and exhale.

3. Continue this breath until your heart's light is encompassing your entire being. Feel yourself surrounded by divine love. Rest here for a few minutes.

4. Invite your guardian angel to come before you and introduce themselves. Don't second-guess or overanalyze; trust whatever name comes to mind and however they appear in your mind's eye, even if it's just as a flash of colored light.

5. In your heart space, ask your guardian angel to assist you with the desires you're currently seeking to manifest. If you feel blocked or need help in specific areas, don't be afraid to share this with them, too.

6. When you're finished with your request, take a moment to sit in their energy. Ask them if they have anything they'd like to share with you. Relax and allow yourself to be open to receiving their wisdom and guidance.

7. When you're complete, thank them for their time and their help. Bring your awareness back into your heart, and feel love and gratitude for your angelic help. Open your eyes when you're ready.

95. Connecting with Your Divine Support Squad

What if you had some otherworldly help with your manifestations? What if there were a consciousness that only knew thoughts of abundance, love, and infinite possibilities, and this consciousness could easily guide you toward the manifestations of your dream life from this higher vantage point? Enter what I lovingly call your *divine support squad*. Whether this squad is made up of angels, guides, ancestors, and deceased loved ones, or you simply relate to it as higher vibrational awareness connected to your own being, this meditation will help you get out-of-this-world help and guidance on your journey.

1. Get your body in a comfortable position, either seated or lying down. Close your eyes and begin to breathe in through your nose and out through your mouth. Feel your whole being relax deeply.

2. Bring your awareness into your heart space. See a ball of golden light there. Watch it glow brightly and expand with each breath you take until it encapsulates your entire body.

3. Feel everything else melt away, except your being in this ball of light. Feel yourself floating up to the ceiling of your room, then up higher to the sky above your home, then even higher, floating above the earth, and even higher yet into the cosmos. Let yourself ascend even higher into a bright, cloud-filled, heaven-like realm.

4. When you arrive at this beautiful spot, you notice a long, white marble table with chairs all around it. There's a seat for you at the head of the table. When you sit down, you call in your divine support squad.

5. Into the room fly the angels, guides, ancestors, deceased loved ones, and any higher beings who are here to assist you in your earth journey. Perhaps you even see your higher self, or more evolved versions of yourself. Welcome whoever shows up at the table, and allow them to introduce themselves.

6. Now share your manifestation intentions with your divine support squad and ask them for any guidance or wisdom they have to share with you on the matter. Sit here for several minutes and simply receive whatever comes forth.

7. When you feel complete, thank them for everything they have shared. Feel yourself descending back down into Earth's atmosphere, down into your city, your home, your room, and, finally, your body. Take several breaths here to reintegrate all you have received. When you're ready, open your eyes. Jot down whatever you want to remember in a journal.

96. Opening Up Your Akashic Records

Think of the Akashic records as the library of the universe, where every thought, interaction, and lifetime we have experienced is logged and categorized. Accessing the Akashic records can help give us greater understanding about why we feel challenged or blocked in certain areas, and then help us release these blocks once they're brought to our awareness. When a manifestation feels stuck, out of reach, or complicated in some way, the records are a great place to go for clarity and forward momentum.

🕐 **10–30 minutes or more**

1. Sit in a relaxed position with your eyes closed, and begin to breathe deeply. Allow any tension or stress to be released from your body on each exhale.

2. On each inhale, imagine bright white, divine light coming into your being and cleaning, clearing, and restoring every cell in your body. On each exhale, continue releasing anything that's no longer serving you. Continue this for several minutes or until you feel like your entire being is full of light.

3. Now request to open the records: "Keepers of the Akashic records, I humbly request guidance, direction, and to know the truth as it is revealed for my highest good and the highest good of all. Help me know myself through the light of the Akashic records and to see myself through the eyes of the Akashic records. Allow me to receive the wisdom and love that my guides, mentors, and loved ones have for me through the knowledge of the Akashic records. The records are now open."

4. In your mind's eye, see a beautiful library in a magical land. Allow whatever first appears to you to be perfect, and move forward to go inside. Find a large book opened at a table in the center of the library. You may even see some of the keepers of the records around it. Walk over and place your hands on the book.

5. Set the intention to be shown whatever is of highest service for your current situation. Trust where your awareness is guided. Allow yourself to go on a journey. If any vows, contracts, or beliefs from other lifetimes may be holding you back, ask the keeper of the records to assist you in releasing them.

6. When you're complete with your journey, say the closing statement: "Thank you to the keepers of the Akashic records and to all my guides, mentors, and loved ones for sharing the wisdom and truth of the Akashic records with me. The records are now closed. The records are now closed. The records are now closed."

7. Gently bring your awareness back to your breath, and allow for a few minutes of integration before you open your eyes and continue your day.

97. Asking for a Sign

Walking the path of manifesting the life you dream of can require a lot of faith. We must believe that things are happening before we see them happening. Asking for a sign can enable us to give the universe, our spirit guides, or a deceased loved one a chance to send us a little wink that everything is working out for us and affirm that we're on the right path. If your faith is being tested or you just want to experience the magic of receiving a sign, this meditation is for you.

1. Begin in a seated position. Close your eyes, and start focusing on your breath. As you inhale and exhale, feel your breath relaxing your entire being.

2. Bring your attention to your heart center. As you breathe into this sacred space, acknowledge what it is on your path that you'd like to receive a sign to affirm. Maybe it's the abundance work you've been doing, that you made the correct decision career-wise, that your loved one is in fact watching over you from the other side— or maybe you just want a general thumbs-up that your manifesting work is in motion.

3. When whatever it is arises in your heart center, set the intention to ask for the sign. Notice if a certain image or form comes to mind as a way you'd like to receive the sign. Acknowledge what comes up, and silently request, "If XYZ is imminent, then please send me this [specific sign] in the next 48 hours."

4. Often, when we open up this communication, the universe, our guides, our loved ones, or simply our intuitive guidance wants to pipe up and share with us a message. Spend several minutes after your request just breathing into your heart space and allowing any messages that may come up for you to be received.

5. When you're complete, thank the universe, your angels, guides, loved ones, the divine, and so on, for sending the sign. Open your eyes, and go about your day, ready for your wink from the universe to appear!

98. Making the Quantum Leap

If you're truly ready to embark on living the life your heart desires, it's likely that you'll come to a "quantum leap" moment (or a few!). Sometimes we metaphorically need to jump from our current mind-set, circumstances, and security blanket into the unknown toward our dreams, with only our faith and belief in ourself as our parachute. This meditation is here to support you through making your quantum leap.

🕐 **10–30 minutes or more**

1. Get into a comfortable position on the floor, on a chair, or on a sofa. You can either sit up or lie down, as long as you won't fall asleep. Close your eyes, and begin focusing on your breath.

2. Allow the leap ahead of you to present itself in all its fear-inducing glory. Just observe it; notice what fears come up, what thoughts attach themselves to it—anything and everything that arises.

3. Now, allow those feelings, thoughts, and ideas to exist while activating your heart center, your space of ultimate truth. Bring your breath and awareness into your heart center with each breath. Just observe what happens to those same fear thoughts and stories.

4. As they begin dissipating and weakening, bring forth the vision and feelings of you after the leap, on the other side, living this new reality. Let the emotions, feelings, and frequency of that vision overpower anything that remains of your fear story.

5. Saturate yourself in the vibration of the post–quantum leap you. Breathe here for several minutes. Feel the trust emanate from your heart, and relax into this impending future.

6. Before you close, ask your heart if there's anything you need to know to prepare yourself for the quantum leap, and get quiet to receive whatever comes up.

7. When you're complete, bring your awareness back into your body. Place your hands on your heart, and close with a few powerful breaths of gratitude for the quantum leap happening in your life.

99. Pineal Gland Activation

Many mystical and spiritual traditions hail the pineal gland as the metaphysical portal between the spirit world and our earthly life. It is a pinecone-sized gland, located in the center of our brain and linked to our body's perception of light. Activating this spiritual center of your being can help us awaken the part of ourselves that already knows we are divine creators.

🕐 10–30 minutes or more

1. Begin in a comfortable, seated position with your eyes closed and your breath slow and deep. Relax your body and quiet your mind.

2. Bring your awareness to the base of your spine. Envision a golden fountain of light originating here. Use your breath and your body to bring the golden light or elixir up your spinal cord until it arrives at the center of your brain, where the pineal gland sits. See the pineal gland and its tiny pinecone-like shape resting in a small chalice, the golden light fluid filling that chalice all the way up and drenching the pineal gland.

3. On each inhale, envision this light moving up your spinal cord and bathing the pineal gland. Once you make it to the chalice, hold your breath and continue to allow the golden light fluid to cover the pineal gland for a few moments.

4. When you can't hold your breath any longer, exhale and allow your whole body to relax.

5. Repeat for another 10 to 15 breaths, or as many as you feel comfortable doing at this point. You may increase the amount of time you can activate it as you continue to practice this work.

6. When you're complete, recline your body to a fully surrendered, lying-down position. Spend the next 10 minutes here with your eyes closed, just being with your breath. Welcome whatever visions, feelings, or experiences want to come through.

100. Connecting with a Loved One on the Other Side

Sometimes our most powerful spiritual helpers are those we loved dearly in life who have passed on. These cherished souls are eager to support us from the spirit world and love being active participants in our manifestations. My grandma, who was very close to me, passed just a month before I signed on to start writing this book. I firmly believe it was her otherworldly assistance that contributed to it manifesting right around my birthday! ;)

🕐 10–30 minutes or more

1. Get into a comfortable, seated position with your eyes closed. Breathe in and out of your heart space.

2. Feel the love for your loved one who has passed well up in your heart. Say their name aloud or silently to yourself, and welcome them into the space with you.

3. Take a moment to feel their presence, their energy, or their essence. You may even see an image of them or a light signature. Trust whatever comes through.

4. Next, simply speak to your loved one. You can tell them how much you miss them, anything in your heart. Be sure to tell them about the vision for your life or what you're currently working on manifesting. Ask them for their help with it!

5. Now sit back and allow yourself to get quiet to receive any wisdom or messages your loved one wants to send to you.

6. When you feel complete with the session, thank your loved one for being with you. If you want, invite them to send you signs as you go about your week to remind you of their presence. Take a few deep breaths, soaking in any guidance and feeling the support of your loved one.

a final word

CONGRATULATIONS! You've made it through! If you've read to this point without putting the meditations into practice, now is the time to go back and start taking action on your manifestation journey. Don't cheat yourself out of the golden keys in this book to unlock your immense creative potential in this life. If you've been meditating as you've gone through the book, huge congrats! I'll bet you're already starting to see major shifts in your life. Showing up for this work has probably brought up beliefs, fears, and perceived limitations that weren't fun to look at, but I'm proud of you for facing them and for moving through them—and I hope you're proud of yourself as well. Don't worry if you feel that you're not doing it perfectly. Be patient and loving with yourself as you begin to feel your manifestations before you start to see them.

Your practice has only just begun. Continue to use this book and its meditations over and over until they become second nature in your life. Each journey through the book and each visit back to a certain meditation will offer you different gifts and transmissions. Your manifestation and meditation practice will only get richer, more magical, and more effortless with your continued commitment. This is the work of our lifetime—this is the deep soul work we came here to do.

It is indeed fun to manifest all sorts of wonderful things for our life, and it's awe-inspiring to see the dreams and desires you've had finally take root in your reality. But the real reward is the *you* that you become on the journey—the happier, more grounded, and more supremely aware of your infinite power and potential *you*. That's what all this is for, right? Becoming the you you've always been deep within, and being a divine co-creator of this wild and precious life you have.

Please stay in touch! Tag me on Instagram or Facebook at @cassandrabodzak with all your pics of your journey using this book to manifest through meditation. I want to celebrate you every step of the way! Check out the Resources list for more information on where you can get your free book bonuses, different ways to go deeper with this work, and how to join my Divinely Design Your Life group program if you want more hands-on help from me.

resources

The *Manifesting through Meditation* Resource Page
CassandraBodzak.com/manifesting
Be sure to visit the book bonus page at CassandraBodzak.com. You'll
find all sorts of bonus content to help you deepen your practice, assist
with your manifesting, and find community with others who are doing
this work as well. You'll also find an extended version of part I of this
text that dives even deeper into the manifesting process and gives you
crucial tools for your journey!

Free Guided Meditation Bundle
DivinelyDesignYourLife.com/meditation-bundle
Need help getting your meditation practice started? This free bundle
contains an AM, PM, and walking meditation to help you get into the
swing of things. A bonus divine visioning meditation is included.

The Unplug Meditation App
This app is great if you're looking for more guided meditations to
help you get into the groove of a daily practice. I have several meditations on the Unplug app, available in all app stores, that can help you
get started.

Free Manifesting Master Class
DivinelyDesignYourLife.com/manifesting-masterclass
Can't get enough information about manifestation? This is perfect for
you! Let me personally share with you the four most common mistakes
that block your manifesting, and my four most powerful tips to amp up
your manifestation practice, in this free virtual workshop.

Divinely Design Your Life
DivinelyDesignYourLife.com
Ready to take things to the next level? Join my signature spiritual
group-coaching program where you'll get the teachings, meditations,

community, and biweekly LIVE calls to support you in making the vision for your life your reality.

Clarity, Miracles, and Momentum Virtual Retreat
CassandraBodzak.teachable.com/p/clarity-miracles
-and-momentum-virtual-retreat
Want to take a weekend at home to go deep, get clear on your vision, and do some powerful work to clear the fears that are blocking you from believing you can manifest it? Check out my *Clarity, Miracles, and Momentum* on-demand virtual retreat for a game-changing weekend.

Eat with Intention: Recipes and Meditations for a Life That Lights You Up
Available wherever books are sold
Is part of your manifesting journey connected to your body and/or self-love? You'll love the meditations, wisdom, and soul-nourishing recipes in my first book.

CRYSTAL365: Crystals for Everyday Life and Your Guide to Health, Wealth, and Balance by Heather Askinosie
For those of you who want to go deeper into using crystals for your meditation practice, this beautiful book makes it easy to learn about different crystals and how to use them.

The Beginner's Guide to Essential Oils: Everything You Need to Know to Get Started by Christina Anthis
If you're ready to dive deeper into essential oils and don't know where to start, this book breaks down 30 essential oils and shows you their properties and how to best use them.

Neville Goddard: The Complete Reader
This collection of works by American mystic Neville Goddard is one of the most powerful texts on manifestation. If you want to learn more as you make your way deeper into your manifestation meditation practice, these classic texts will be invaluable.

Florence Scovel Shinn: The Complete Works
If you want to dive deeper into the power of your words as it relates to creating your reality, Florence Scovel Shinn, who famously wrote "Your words are your wands," is a wealth of information.

Creative Visualization by Shakti Gawain
This is a great book, whether you're struggling with visualization in your practice or simply want to take it to the next level. Shakti Gawain breaks down the power of visualization for manifestation and provides lots of exercises to try it.

Becoming Supernatural by Dr. Joe Dispenza
If you're struggling with a health condition and using manifestation to create healing or perfect well-being, this book will provide you with tools to go even deeper on your journey, along with stories of miraculous healing to empower you along the way.

from the author

Listen to my podcast *Divine Downloads* on iTunes, Spotify, Google Podcasts, IHeartRadio, YouTube, and any other place your favorite podcasts play!

If you loved the spiritual concepts and manifestation wisdom in this book, you'll really enjoy the interviews and deep-dive solo-casts on the podcast. Use it as a way to continue going deeper and staying inspired on your manifestation journey.

Get Manifestation "Text Support" from Me
my.community.com/CassandraBodzak
Want texts from me to cheer you on and remind you of key things on your manifesting journey? Sign up to get sporadic reminders from me straight to your phone.

Ask Me Anything! (and receive a short video message back)
HeyHero.com/influencer/CassandraBodzak
Since my spots for one-on-one coaching fill up so fast, this brilliant new website provides a solution for when you just have that one burning question for me. Ask away, and I'll help you get to the next step on your journey with a personalized response via video.

Follow Me on Social Media
I put out tons of free content through my social media and YouTube channel each week—everything from live talks to guided meditations and tools for divinely designing your life.

instagram.com/cassandrabodzak

facebook.com/cassandrabodzak

youtube.com/cassandrabodzakTV

tiktok.com/cassandrabodzak

clubhouse: @cassandrabodzak

CassandraBodzak.com/MeditationsforManifesting

@cassandrabodzak on Instagram

references

Aman, Mansoor M. "Evidence-Based Non-Pharmacological Therapies for Fibromyalgia." Accessed April 14, 2021. https://pubmed.ncbi.nlm.nih.gov/29619620.

Cearley, Shannon, M., et al. "Irritable Bowel Syndrome: The Effect of FODMAPs and Meditation on Pain Management." Accessed April 14, 2021. https://www.sciencedirect.com/science/article/abs/pii/S1876382017301014.

Goyal, Madhav, et al. "Meditation Programs for Psychological Stress and Well-Being: A Systematic Review and Meta-Analysis." Accessed April 14, 2021. https://pubmed.ncbi.nlm.nih.gov/24395196.

Hilton, Lara, et al. "Meditation for Posttraumatic Stress: Systematic Review and Meta-Analysis." Accessed April 14, 2021. https://pubmed.ncbi.nlm.nih.gov/27537781.

Hofmann, Stefan G. and Angelina F. Gómez. "Mindfulness-Based Interventions for Anxiety and Depression." Accessed April 14, 2021. https://www.ncbi.nlm.nih.gov/pmc/articles/PMC5679245.

Merriam-Webster Online. "Meditate." Accessed April 14, 2021. https://www.merriam-webster.com/dictionary/meditate.

Rosenkranz, Mellisa A., et al. "A Comparison of Mindfulness-Based Stress Reduction and an Active Control in Modulation of Neurogenic Inflammation." Accessed April 14, 2021. https://www.sciencedirect.com/science/article/abs/pii/S0889159112004758.

Schucman, Helen. *A Course in Miracles*. Glen Elen, CA: Foundation for Inner Peace, 1992.

Tong, Yingge, et al. "Effects of Tai Chi on Self-Efficacy: A Systematic Review." Accessed April 14, 2021. https://www.ncbi.nlm.nih.gov/pmc/articles/PMC6114250.

index

R

S

T

U

V

W